Southill and the Whitbreads

1795 – 1995

A collection of essays
to celebrate two centuries
of Southill House and Estate
in the hands of the
Whitbread family

Editor: Patricia Bell

1995

© S. C. Whitbread
1995
Reprinted 2009

ISBN 0 9526945 0 6

Published by S. C. Whitbread, Southill Park, Biggleswade, Bedfordshire SG18 9LL

Designed and printed by Stanley L. Hunt (Printers) Ltd, Midland Road, Rushden, Northants

Contents

	List of illustrations	4
	Contributors	5
	Acknowledgements	6
	Foreword *by* Sam Whitbread	9
1	Samuel Whitbread I *by* Simon Houfe	11
2	Southill and the Byngs *by* Patricia Bell	16
3	Southill House *by* Andrew Brookes	24
4	The Estate and the Enclosure Movement *by* Norman Parry	31
5	Southill – A Sporting Estate *by* Sam Whitbread and Stephen Bunker	39
6	Church and School Life *by* Joan Curran	52
7	Whitbread Monuments and Memorials *by* Linda Swain	69
8	The Midland Railway *by* Martin Lawrence	77
9	Southill at War *by* Carol Parry	88
10	Southill Estate Buildings – an Architectural Tour *by* Bernard West	97
11	The Trees and Woodland *by* John Niles	111
12	The Estate Today *by* Sam Whitbread	120

List of Illustrations

		Page
1	Samuel Whitbread I by Sir Joshua Reynolds, 1786	10
2	Southill Park – from an engraving by Thomas Badeslade, c.1739	19
3	Southill House, from an engraving by W. Watts, 1782	20
4	Samuel Whitbread II by John Opie, 1804	25
5	The Rebuilding of Southill in 1797 by George Garrard (**also cover**)	28
6	Henry Holland, bust by George Garrard	29
7	Cartouche from the Henlow Enclosure Award Map 1798	35
8	Southill Gamekeepers c.1930	43
9	Samuel Howard Whitbread's 80th Birthday shoot, 1938	46
10	Memorial to Charles Dines, shot by poachers in 1815	49
11	Cricket at Southill, by Thomas Jackson 1886	50
12	Southill Lower School, by Bernard West	54
13	Elstow Bunyan Meeting Sunday School Treat, 1906	58
14	Children on Elstow Green	60
15	Broom Methodist Chapel, once the school	67
16	Memorial to Samuel Whitbread I in Cardington Church	70
17	Memorial to William Charles Whitbread in Cardington Church	71
18	Memorial to Samuel Whitbread II and the Wedgwood Font, in Cardington Church by Bernard West	73
19	William Henry Whitbread, by William Bradley 1841	78
20	Southill Station, 1969	81
21	Obelisk to William Henry Whitbread, Keepers' Warren	84
22	The Queen inspecting Southill Red Cross, Gastlings 1943	93
23	Bomb damage at Broom Crossroads, 1940	94
24	VE Day Party at Southill School, 1945	95
25	Workmen employed on the rebuilding of Elstow Church 1880-82	98
26	Elstow Church restoration, by Thomas Jobson Jackson 1880	99
27	Cardington Church before rebuilding began in 1897	100
28	School Lane, Southill, by Bernard West	103
29	Harrowden Lane, by Bernard West	105
30	Cardington Green, by Bernard West	106
31	Howard Reading Room, Cardington, by Bernard West	107
32	The Little House, Cardington, by Bernard West	109
33	Plan of part of Exeter and Great Warden Woods, August 1843	112
34	Triangles and diamonds along the Southill hedgerows, 1826	116
35	Timber waggons near Cotton End, c.1930	118
36	Southill Garden Party, June 1995	121
37	Presentation of Bledisloe Gold Medal to Sam Whitbread, 1989	122

Contributors

Patricia Bell was County Archivist at the Bedfordshire County Record Office from 1968-1986, and general editor of the *Bedfordshire Historical Record Society* from 1978-1991.

Andrew Brookes, partner with the conservation practice, Rodney Melville and Partners, Architects, was partner in charge of the recent restoration at Southill House.

Stephen Bunker, Senior Lecturer in History at the University of Luton, was Keeper of Local History at Luton Museum 1982-1993, and former chairman of Luton Historical Society.

Joan Curran of Totternhoe, a chartered librarian, before retirement worked in the school library service at Manshead Upper School. Secretary and founder member of the Dunstable and District Local History Society.

Simon Houfe, art historian and biographer, was on the staff of the Victoria & Albert Museum before working as an editor. He lives in Bedfordshire where he was born.

Martin Lawrence, once head of history at a Bedfordshire High School, now partner in a firm of occupational psychologists, formed Harlington Heritage Trust in 1981 and is now chairman of the Bedfordshire Local History Association.

John Niles, born in Devon, worked with the Forestry Commission, and has been Trees and Woodland Officer in the Planning Department of the Bedfordshire County Council since 1973.

Carol Parry, born in Bedfordshire, is a professional archivist who has worked at Leicestershire and Bedfordshire County Record Offices. She has also taught local history to adults.

Norman Parry of Potton came to Bedfordshire in 1972 after a career in the RAF. Founder member and past chairman of the Potton History Society.

Linda Swain, a retired teacher from Essex, has lived since 1982 in Toddington. Member of Toddington Historical Society and a NADFAS church recorder.

Bernard West, architect, born and educated in Bedford, worked in London and for 30 years in his home town, specialising in rehabilitation and restoration. Well known as an artist and naturalist.

Acknowledgements

Illustrations are reproduced by kind permission of the Bedfordshire County Record Office (7, 13, 14, 15, 20, 25, 27, 35); Mrs Cynthia Clarke (8, 9); Bernard West (12, 28, 29, 30, 31, 32); and Mr Arthur Massey and *The Bedfordshire Times* (22, 23, 24). I am grateful to the Royal Agricultural Society for permission to reprint the extract from their *Journal* which appears on page 123.

S.C.W.

The Whitbreads

AN OUTLINE FAMILY TREE

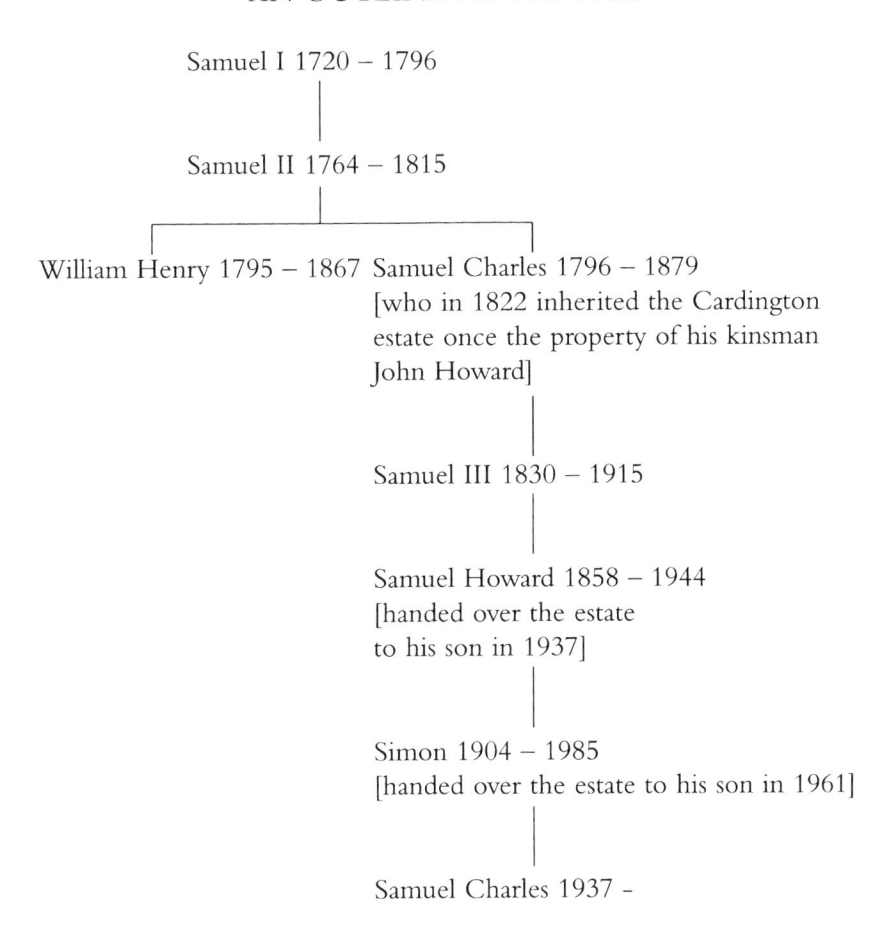

Samuel I 1720 – 1796

Samuel II 1764 – 1815

William Henry 1795 – 1867

Samuel Charles 1796 – 1879
[who in 1822 inherited the Cardington estate once the property of his kinsman John Howard]

Samuel III 1830 – 1915

Samuel Howard 1858 – 1944
[handed over the estate to his son in 1937]

Simon 1904 – 1985
[handed over the estate to his son in 1961]

Samuel Charles 1937 -

Foreword

On 20 June 1795 Samuel Whitbread I signed the final conveyance which delivered to him Southill Park and the surrounding estate from their previous owner, the 4th Viscount Torrington. The purchase of Southill put in place the final piece of the jigsaw of land purchases on which Samuel Whitbread had embarked in the 1780s.

To mark the 200th anniversary of this last, and most significant, acquisition, I have invited a group of local historians under the leadership of the chairman of the Bedfordshire Local History Association, Martin Lawrence, to contribute a number of essays on various aspects of the Southill Estate during the past 200 years. The volume should in no way be looked on as an estate history. Rather, it is a series of studies, each complete in itself, of individual subjects relating to the estate over this period, drawing heavily on the family archives deposited in the Bedfordshire County Record Office. These records in no way give a complete picture of the Southill Estate or its owners. For instance, although there is copious manuscript material for the life of Samuel Whitbread II (1764-1815), if you were to use only the documents in the Record Office, in the words of the Editor "the Whitbreads apparently ceased to exist" during the Victorian era.

My thanks are due to all the contributors who have given unsparingly of their time and knowledge, for no reward except the pleasure of the work. It is my hope that they have enjoyed the exercise; they can certainly feel justly proud of the result.

Chris Pickford, the County Archivist, has together with his staff given much assistance and guidance to the contributors, and his knowledge of publishing matters has been invaluable to me.

However, the whole project would not have been possible without the help and enthusiasm of Patricia Bell, Chris Pickford's distinguished predecessor as County Archivist, who willingly assumed the mantle of Editor, and who, with firm but gentle cajoling, has extracted from each author his or her contribution on time, and has wielded the editorial blue pencil with tact and discretion. To her, above all, is credit due for any pleasure that may be derived from this volume.

As will be seen, much has inevitably changed over two centuries, but I like to think that the principles by which the first Samuel Whitbread conducted his personal and business life run as a thread through the story of the past 200 years. My hope is that the Estate will continue to thrive in the hands of the family for many years to come.

SAM WHITBREAD, Southill, July 1995

Samuel Whitbread I by Sir Joshua Reynolds, 1786

Chapter 1

Samuel Whitbread I

by SIMON HOUFE

A SENSE OF HISTORY and a sense of place are important for any man returning to his roots. Samuel Whitbread I (1720-1796) had them both in abundance. From 1760 Whitbread was purchasing land in Bedfordshire, the beginning of a plan which with patience and foresight was to create one of the greatest estates in the county.

The Whitbreads had their origins in this part of England. William Whitbread was established at Ion (Eyon) House, Gravenhurst, in the early seventeenth century. Ion House was a substantial manor, as can be seen from the beautiful watercolours of Thomas Fisher, and the Whitbreads were a minor gentry family of considerable influence. William Whitbread had bought land at Cardington, south-east of Bedford, in 1639, and his son Henry moved there in about 1650. These facts are recorded by his great-grandson, Samuel Whitbread I, in his brief memoir (1788).

William Whitbread of Cardington, Henry's son and the brewer's grandfather, was a staunch supporter of the Parliamentarians in the Civil War, and in 1653 he and his wife Lettice joined the congregation of the saintly John Gifford at Bedford (now Bunyan Meeting) at the same time as John Bunyan. This dedication and serious concern in religious matters continued with his son Henry Whitbread (1664-1727), a Receiver General for Land Taxes in Bedfordshire. He and his first wife Sarah Ive, from a wealthy London merchant family, also sought church membership. They were all nonconformist tradespeople, connected to the City, and with a strong protestant belief in hard work and improvement.

Samuel Whitbread I was born at Cardington in 1720, the youngest son of Henry Whitbread by his second wife Elizabeth Winch, a widow, née Read. His father died in 1727, but left the boy well provided for. According to the memoir of Mrs Gordon, his daughter, Samuel was educated "at a Clergyman's in Northamptonshire" and in 1736 his widowed mother placed him as apprentice to a leading London brewer. By 1742, while still in his early twenties, he used his patrimony to go into partnership with two brothers called Shewell, and between them they purchased a small brewery. He bought the surviving partner out in 1761, and by then the brewery was on a site in Chiswell Street. His relations with members of his staff were always exceptionally warm. He personally ordered that his associates' portraits should be painted for his house, a remarkable testimony of regard. Mrs Gordon's memoir gives a good impression of the young man at this period. "... In the early part of his Trade he sat up in a chair four nights in a week by the Side of his Brewhouse Coppers, refreshed himself by washing plentifully with cold Water, a clean Shirt, and When the State of the Boiling permitting his quitting, retired for 2 hours to his closet reading the Scriptures and Devotional Exercises". Somehow, this picture gives an impression of Hogarth's 'Industrious Apprentice' fulfilling all his father's wishes and prospering in the City of London.

Whitbread was not only hard working but extremely wise, his caution leading him to eschew any speculating in the unstable markets of Georgian London. His daughter recalled "tho' often Solicited to take Shares in Banking Houses by which so many have of Late Suffered, as he said, if a Man does not *know* a business He should not go into it". Whitbread concentrated his energies on his brewing establishment in Chiswell Street. It prospered greatly in the 1760s and 1770s and by the 1790s was the largest in the land with an annual output of 200,000 barrels, and with capital of £250,000. A man of Whitbread's convictions was also anxious to serve his country, and the best way that he could do that was by serving Bedfordshire.

From 1761 he had been acquiring land in the parish of Cardington. Recalling this in 1788 he wrote "I bought at Cardington because it was the place of my birth and inheritance of my Fathers – And as it has pleased God to bless me with good abundance who went out as Jacob said 'with my staff only' (for my patrimony was only £2000, being the seventh of eight Children and youngest of five sons)". He went on to say that he felt it was his duty to show gratitude "by improving the place I was born in, & the Parish where our Family have lived 150 Years" and "to make it more acceptable to my Children & their posterity". He had also acquired land in the parishes of Shillington and Lower Gravenhurst, because of the family's long connection with Ion House in Gravenhurst.

It is interesting to note that Whitbread did not embark on these purchases for historical or sentimental reasons only. On the contrary, when he was negotiating for the purchase of the lease of the great tithes of Cardington belonging to Trinity College Cambridge, he cross-questioned a local farmer on their economic viability. He desired to know the charge for highway tolls, the amount of poor rates, the cost of transporting grain and whether threshing and loading charges could be offset by profit from straw, hogs and pigeons. With the great tithes went the range of tithe barns and the adjoining house, Fenlake Barns, which he and his family used when visiting Bedford.

In 1767 Samuel Whitbread showed interest in contesting one of the two parliamentary seats for the borough of Bedford, a seat that was controlled by the Duke of Bedford's faction. This brought him into conflict with the 4th Duke, but by 1768 Whitbread had come to an agreement with the Duke and was elected along with the Duke's candidate. The alliance between the Russells and the Whitbreads as prominent Whig families (and also with the Ossorys and the Antonies) was to last for years, making the Whig dominance in Bedfordshire one of the most remarkable in England. Samuel Whitbread I was elected again in 1774 after a dispute over irregularities and this was followed by victories in 1780 and 1784. He only retired in 1790 in favour of his son, having become a well respected figure in the town and having established a great following for his family in the political race. A county seat, a more contentious challenge, depended largely on aristocratic patronage and it was thought inadvisable for the London brewer to contest this.

It was probably a wise move, for Whitbread did not want to meet an aristocratic challenge while he was establishing his credentials. The reason that he was so well accepted in the county was almost certainly his pragmatic approach, his gradual build up of acreage over the years, and the fact that his ancestors were associated with both borough and county. By the 1770s he was not only well known in Bedford but his relationship with John Howard and other small landowners in Bedfordshire and Buckinghamshire would have been appreciated. These were not the predatory moves of an outsider, but of a successful son who was returning home.

Apart from his immensely successful business enterprises, Whitbread was as much of a reformer as his cousin John Howard. Mrs Gordon records in her memoir that he was a foremost advocate for the abolition of slavery. She writes "He really was the first man who mentioned the Slave Trade in the House of Commons and called Mr Pitts attention to it . . . ". Both Mrs Gordon and her sister Lady St John of Bletsoe were ardent reformers and the whole family moved in the circle of William Wilberforce, and Lady St John in particular was involved in the evangelical Moravian church. Mrs Gordon records the first moves towards the abolition of slavery, "the Early and Small Meetings of the Friends to Enquire into the Trade were held in the Drawing Room at my Father's in Portman Sq.. There came Sir Wm Dalben, and the Great Spring of that, has or ever will follow to break the Chain of Slavery that Worthy humble Excellent Man & Scholar

Granville Sharp. . . ". Harriot Gordon acted as her father's amanuensis on these occasions, writing down everything that occurred. Whitbread invited the famous abolitionist Thomas Clarkson (1760-1846) to stay in his house, where he supported him for several months. Mrs Gordon comments on the fact that there is no mention of Whitbread in Clarkson's *History of the Abolition of The Slave Trade*. She concludes that it was because the self-effacing Whitbread did not wish it! This is borne out by a very interesting inscription by Clarkson in an 1808 edition of his book in the library at Southill, in which he states his indebtedness to both Whitbreads, father and son. "To Samuel Whitbread Esq. an able and zealous advocate in Parliament in the great cause of the Abolition of the Slave Trade and the descendant of a Father who perseveringly during his Life-time gave it his most substantial Support, this Work is affectionately presented by The Author."

Samuel Whitbread I had acquired the Hertfordshire estate of Bedwell Park in Essendon in 1765 as his country seat, and also Woolmers, a pleasant house nearby. There he lived the life of a country gentleman with his second wife, Lady Mary Whitbread, a daughter of Earl Cornwallis. He spent the summers at Bedwell, returning to his business in London in the winter and spring. Mrs Gordon gives a glimpse of this idyllic life at Bedwell. "The Spot his Wife and he had mutually chosen was in itself very pretty uncommonly well timbered with Old Oaks Elms Spanish Chestnuts . . . as you drove in at the Gate and up the road threw a Double Avenue of Oaks on a Sunny Evening from the bustle of London [it] had most captivating charms for such a mind as his, and he never lost a vacant opportunity of repairing thither, If as he said but to breath fresh-air in the night."

Whitbread remained extremely active until his seventies as is recalled by one of his staff. "It was the custom with old Mr Whitbread, during the Autumn Months, when he was residing at Bedwell Park, to go once a week or oftener, up to his Brewhouse in Chiswell Street, and as he seldom took any dinner, his tea was a meal, and sitting in his large Parlour, which adjoined his inner Counting-house in which sat the head Clerks, which led into the outer Counting-house in which were the others, to have the head Clerks in by turns, to converse with, and the youngest clerk, a lad about 18, to read the Newspaper of the day loud."

The two best portraits of Samuel Whitbread I date from this decade of his life and are by Sir Joshua Reynolds and Sir William Beechey. Although the Reynolds is a more animated portrait, showing the brewer with his inkstand at his side and his papers spread on a table, the Beechey seems more penetrating. This portrait has nothing to distract from the close wig, the plain coat and the set but benevolent face of the philanthropist and man of business. One can appreciate from this why Whitbread's great objects in the county were the creation of a new county prison instead of the old, insanitary gaol, the setting up of a county infirmary and the creation of Sunday Schools.

Samuel Whitbread I wanted the best for his children, especially for his only son, whom he would have liked to take over at the brewery. However, he had given the younger Samuel an education where his friends were future landowners and politicians, and this was the life the son wanted for himself. It was this that led him to buy the Southill estate in 1795, thereby consolidating the family's presence in Bedfordshire. Stricken by paralysis in 1793, Samuel must have felt that this was a crowning achievement. When he died at Bedwell Park on 11 June 1796 the newspapers described him as "universally known and lamented".

Chapter 2

Southill and the Byngs

by PATRICIA BELL

THE GRAVEL BEDS on the west bank of the River Ivel have always attracted settlers. Celtic Britons were farming there when the Romans built the Great North Road and, when the Romans had left and many of the early inhabitants had been driven out by the Anglo-Saxon invaders, we find the Gifle tribe giving their name to what were later the villages of Northill and Southill (North Gifle and South Gifle), on either side of Warden, the lookout hill. All three parishes were composed of a number of hamlets or 'ends', and in Southill we find Broom, Stanford or Duxall End, East End, Church End, Ireland and West End. In the eighteenth century West End, which lay a little to the west of the present Southill House, was swallowed up in Southill Park. In addition there were the outlying manor houses of Gastlings and Rowney.

The Great North Road allowed easy access to London, a main market, and this could have encouraged market gardening to develop from the early seventeenth century on the river gravels along the River Ivel in the east of the parishes. In the west the ground rises to an area of wooded sandstone hills. It seems likely that the road helped also to attract the many prosperous families who wanted a country house in an area of light soil where there were woods and spinneys. In the middle ages, before rabbits had become acclimatized, rabbit warrens were established on the sandy soil at Rowney and Warden and, until they became a pest, these would have been an added attraction, both for sport and for fresh meat. From the late sixteenth century an unusual number of gentry families settled in the three parishes. The little wooded hills screened each from his neighbours, yet a relatively large number of gentlefolk in a small area allowed for a more lively social life.

Some of the families, such as the Harveys, lasted for two or three centuries; some had a briefer stay. One notable resident was Lord Chief Justice Kelyng, the judge who showed little kindness to John Bunyan and his wife when the former was brought before him at the Assizes in Bedford. John Kelyng came from a legal family based at Hertford and the family had owned a small farm in Southill since well before the Civil War. Kelyng married Martha Boteler, of the Boteler family of Biddenham, which was one of those deeply divided during the Civil War. Martha's eldest brother, Sir William Boteler, was the leader of the Parliamentarians in the county; a younger brother, Francis, fought for the king. John Kelyng himself was a royalist who was imprisoned and had his property sequestrated during the Commonwealth.

If the family's first purchase had been an investment, after the Restoration, when John Kelyng returned to a successful legal career, he continued to buy up property in Southill because he wished to have his country seat there. This property his son, another John, inherited on his father's death in 1671.

There had been several purchases, the main one being the manor of Gastlings with 200 acres of land, but Judge Kelyng also bought a capital messuage or mansion house formerly occupied by Sir Henry Massingberd, and with this went several fields including Over Dansy Bowers and Nether Dansy Bowers. The house and land was probably the old rectory estate. A map of 1777 shows that Over and Nether Dansy Bowers lay down the east side of the present park. The site of this house is indicated in an early title deed conveying a house which adjoined the churchyard on the east and the dwelling house of John Kelyng on the north, so it is clear that the mansion house lay a little north-west of the church.

George Byng, later created Viscount Torrington, was of an impoverished gentry family from Kent but he made his career in the navy and ended as an admiral with a considerable fortune from prize money. In his youth he had often stayed at Everton, his mother's home, and he too was attracted by Southill, and from 1693 began to buy up property, much of it having once belonged to the Kelyngs. His first purchase was the mansion house near the church.

When, in his son's marriage settlement of 1724, George Viscount Torrington made provision for his own wife, he gave her a life interest in the mansion house where he himself then lived. In his will made 8 July 1732, he left to her instead a life interest in his capital messuage newly erected "at some little distance from the old one pulled down". Possibly the new house was being built in September 1725, when Torrington (staying at Chicksands, the country house of the Osborn family) wrote to his daughter Sarah Osborn in London "Your Mother grows younger and younger, Rides out a Setting, is fond of the fields, and Calls all the patridges hers, her new house pleases her Too, so That in the Main she seems to be as easie and happie as any Wife I know, and belive she thinks so Too".

As Viscount Torrington pursued his aim of having a handsome new-built mansion in an equally handsome park, the old mansion house was demolished and its site absorbed into the new gardens. A note says that the old house "stood where a pond now is in the shrubbery". In the autumn of 1725 Torrington was asking the family at Wrest Park and Mr Bromsall of Northill for young trees. "The size I want I coud have At the Nurseries about London for 12d a peece, but the Carriage would be Intollerable". He asked his neighbours to let him buy small elms and hornbeam from the thickets of underwood, "The size of the stems about the bigness of ones Wrist", though in his next letter he said that he now thought he would not be ready to start planting that year. A year later, in a letter to Sarah Osborn from Southill in November 1726, he wrote "I wont trouble you with our affairs at Southill... and I only at this time tell you youl be Wellcome when you see it (your Name is Writ over the Door)". This could indicate that the new house was finished and occupied.

The thumbnail sketch of the new house on William Gordon's printed map of Bedfordshire of 1736 is in essentials the same as the building shown in Thomas Badeslade's print of c. 1739 and in the 1782 engraving.

Around the new mansion the park began to take shape, for Byng had bought up many of the properties later included within its bounds. Gordon's map shows an ornamental plantation round the house but the same convention is used also for Warden Warren, so probably he meant by this to indicate an area used for recreation. At the end of a northern vista is an obelisk.

The next evidence, Thomas Badeslade's print, shows a road system very different from today's. The road to Warden from the village centre ran northwards parallel to the present road but west of the church, so it was within the area of today's park and was then the park's eastern boundary. North of Southill House Badeslade shows a large rectangle of lawn edged with blocks of shrubbery cut by geometrically designed irregular paths which ran between tall clipped hedges, perhaps box or even the hornbeam Torrington had bought from his neighbours. Running north and south against the west side of the lawn is an artificial canal, arrow straight, with an octagonal pond at its northern end and an unlinked circular pond to the south. The line of the canal was continued north by an avenue of trees at the end of which was an obelisk. In the east border of the lawn and not far from the church was a large artificial mound. It is possible that Badeslade's print was a little idealised but it certainly showed Viscount Torrington's work. In 1793 John Byng, grandson of the first Viscount, wrote somewhat acidly in his diary of the cost of both. "My grandfather thus built Southill House in an open field; and had to plant trees, to dig canals, to make mounts, and to throw away his money in vile taste", and he went on to say that

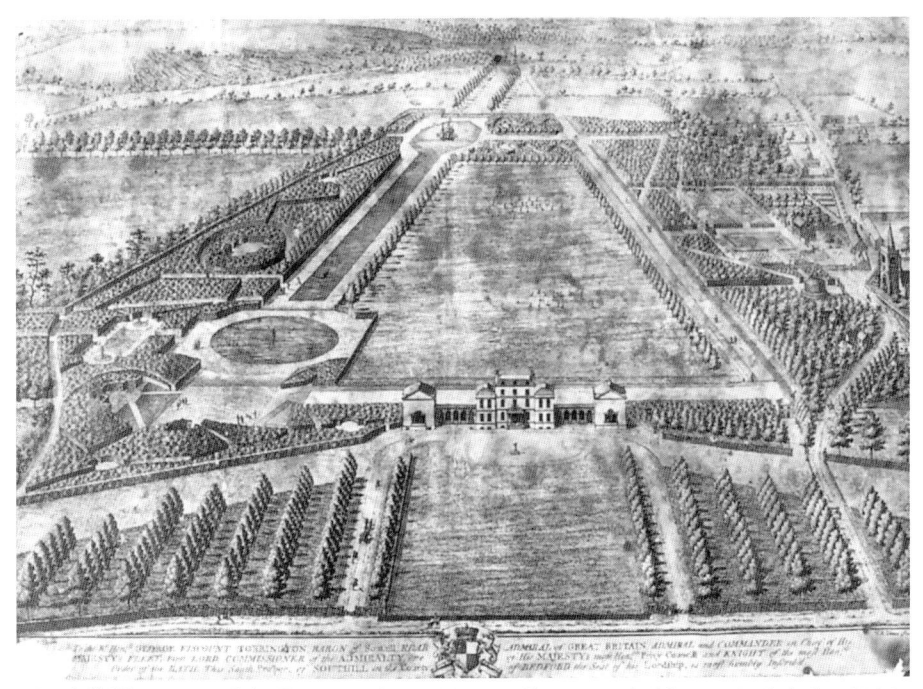

Southill House, seat of the Rt. Hon. George Viscount Torrington, by Thomas Badeslade c.1739

both his "grandfather admiral and my uncle admiral would, from folly and pride, rear places, and they both died ere they were finish'd, leaving their heirs encumber'd with great houses and inadequate estates". South of the house was a semicircular entrance drive enclosing a small lawn with formal plantations either side. Both entrances to the drive joined the road which then ran from Southill village through Southill Warren to Deadman's Cross. This road then ran due west from the village centre straight across the present park and was then the park's southern border.

The design of his park pleased Torrington, but soon seemed old fashioned. In May 1745 Catherine Talbot, a well educated young woman, was staying at Wrest Park with her childhood friends Mary Grey and Jemima Campbell. One day they all visited Southill Park. "The place upon the whole worth seeing; several long pleasant rooms and several agreable pictures done in Italy, though by no top hand; some views of Messina, Naples, Gibraltar and many other places where the late lord had the command of the fleet were exceedingly amusing and finely done; the gardens of 50 acres, but too formal and not ornamented in a good taste".

Southill House, 1782
from an engraving by W. Watts for his "Seats of the Nobility and Gentry"

Jefferys' map of c. 1765 confirms the old road lay-out and he shows a paling fence around an area of about 60 acres of park north of the house. There is no indication of what lay within the park except for an avenue of trees which ran north from the house, ending at a building – perhaps a tower – near where the stream was later dammed to form the lake.

The great change came in 1777 when a much larger park was redesigned by Lancelot 'Capability' Brown. However hampered the Byngs were financially, the park was now to follow fashion and be turned into a carefully designed natural landscape. From an estate map of 1777, the canal with its north and south ponds had gone; the ground to the north of the house has no avenue of trees, and is apparently natural pasture and wood. Work had not yet begun on the lake. The road to Deadman's Cross has already been diverted, unofficially, and south of the house there are now about 50 or 60 acres of open parkland, cut through by a long drive or avenue. This would have been the park seen by John Byng as he rode out from the Sun Inn at Biggleswade later in the century. He was a friend and admirer of Lancelot Brown so he did not regret the money spent on Brown's designs, or on the work needed to carry them out.

It could be that this was the final extravagance that brought the fourth Viscount to bankruptcy. We know that he paid 'Capability' Brown £500 in 1777 for George Bowstreed, Brown's foreman, to supervise the work at Southill, but this would have been a small sum compared with the cost of labour and materials to reshape a whole landscape. The Byng family had overreached themselves financially, and the situation was beyond remedy. George, the fourth Viscount, was in debt for £94,000 and was besieged by creditors. His friends, led by the Duke of Portland, became trustees of his estates, to see if there might be a way to rescue him.

In 1779 Amabel, wife of Lord Polwarth, wrote to her mother, the Marchioness Grey of Wrest Park. The young couple wanted to rent Southill, which could be had fully furnished, needing only linen and china. They were surprised to hear from a friend of the Duke of Portland that they could rent the house for £100 a year and the cautious Lord Polwarth wrote to the Duke to make absolutely sure that no other creditors could disturb his tenancy. Amabel described the arrangement of the rooms on the different floors and went on "The most curious part is a new Range of low offices that were scarcely finish'd when Lord T left England", which suggests that Torrington had fled abroad to avoid his creditors. Amabel continued "There is also an unfinish'd Bath where the Workmen seem to have been sent away at a Minute's Warning, for the very Mortar is lying ready to join some tottering Bricks. Indeed there are Materials enough to philosophize for an Hour ... for I never saw a House where the Warning against Extravagance was more complete".

When Lord and Lady Polwarth took the tenancy a full inventory was made of the rooms and their contents. Earlier Lord Polwarth, a keen sportsman, had spoken scathingly of the layout of the house, but added "It is a charming place out of doors, and fine running about". Alas, Polwarth died in the spring of 1781 and the family's steward needed to dispose of the rest of the lease. He sent for approval a draft of the advertisement:

"To be let and Enterd on immediately,
That substantial well built Capital Mansion call'd Southill House with all necessary and Convenient Offices etc., and is fit for the reception of a Large Family, together with a large and well-planted Kitchen Garden in which are Two Hot Houses and One Green House. The Mansion is Elegantly Furnished and situate on an Exceeding dry Healthy and pleasant Spot, surrounded with about Eighty

Acres of fine Rich pasture ground which may be had with the House, is Very near a Good Turnpike Road from London to Bedford, is 44 Miles from the Former and 7 from the latter, 4 Miles from Biggleswade, 3 Miles from Shefford and in the Pleasantest and most desirable part of the County of Bedford."

John Byng, the diarist and penurious younger brother of the fourth Viscount, thought himself "form'd for a quiet county gentleman, to be idly busied in farming, planting and gardening" and "fishing, riding, and in reading old and new authors". However, he had only small private means and after a spell in the army, he obtained a position at the Stamp Office in London. But he loved Southill and when he took his country holidays at the Sun Inn, Biggleswade, on most days "my ride after breakfast is generally about Southill, not only for the recurrence of the memory of my youth, and the many happy days passed there, but as the soil is so dry and the views very beautiful". Sometimes he went rabbitting in Southill Warren, and in 1790 he described the Gothic Lodge put up by his brother (the fourth Viscount). "Lord T. disfigured the country by building some of the strangest illfashioned buildings that ever were conceiv'd; and tho' in the constant waste of money, and pursuit of taste, Never produced anything of beauty or utility!". In 1791 as Byng rode through Southill on his way back to Biggleswade, he saw Lord Euston, the then tenant, walking before the house, and in 1794 Byng ventured into the menagerie, "wild, over-grown", to cut himself a walking stick from the stem of a guelder-rose. He inherited the title in 1812 but he never owned Southill House, which by then had belonged to the Whitbreads for seventeen years.

As we have seen, the first Samuel Whitbread came from an established family of minor gentry in the county and had amassed a considerable fortune from the profits of his London brewery. He had hoped that his son, the younger Samuel, who came of age in 1785, would take on the management of the brewery but Samuel II was determined on a career in politics and had no interest in the family firm.

It took the elder Samuel a little time to accept this decision but he then set about providing a good base for his son's political career. The father had always considered that land was the only safe investment for profits from his brewery "English land is the only security, and best to live on the income of it if proprietors will submit to the interest it brings, which scarce any body will do". Though he had by now bought up over 2,200 acres in Bedfordshire (mainly in Cardington, Old Warden and Shillington), much of his invested capital was in land in Wiltshire, Essex and Kent, and this was sold in order to extend the Bedfordshire holdings. Political power in a county came from a large acreage in that county, good tenants and a central mansion house for entertaining, as the St Johns had at Melchbourne and the Russell family at Woburn.

In 1794 Samuel Whitbread senior lent the Byngs £7,500 and on 20 June 1795 he purchased the Byng estates in Southill and Old Warden for £85,500. Southill suited the Whitbread family's needs exactly. The handsome house in an attractive park had with it over 3500 acres of land which adjoined or was near to land already owned by Samuel Whitbread I and the purchase more than doubled his previous acreage in the county. By the time of the elder Samuel's death in 1796 his Bedfordshire estate was over 8,000 acres, making it in extent second only to the Woburn estate of the Dukes of Bedford.

It is likely that John Byng, the diarist, would not have been too unhappy when he heard of the sale. In 1790 he wrote that he had ridden "to where the priory of Warden till very lately remained in good preservation; but now nothing but a back part of the offices remain preserv'd, as the whole would have been by the late purchaser, Mr Whitbread, had he come in time (being an improver and preserver)". The early purchases in Old Warden had once been the property of the Palmer and Wasse families but soon the Whitbreads had procured the enclosure of both Southill and Old Warden, which allowed the Ongleys of Old Warden and the Whitbreads of Southill to exchange land and so consolidate their property in their own villages. There would be further purchases but the Southill estate was now the Whitbread family's base.

Chapter 3

Southill House

by ANDREW BROOKES

THE HOUSE AT Southill Park is widely acclaimed as the masterpiece of the architect Henry Holland. While externally the architecture has become blurred by both passage of time and by inappropriate repairs, particularly in the 1960s, the interiors survive almost unaltered as a perfect example of the complete Regency house. As a reaction, perhaps, to the flamboyance of the baroque style of the early house, Holland's style, perfected at Southill, is a statement or perhaps more accurately an understatement of restraint in architectural form and decorative detailing.

Henry Holland was born in London on 20 July 1745. The son of a Master Builder, Holland learned his trade in the family business. Holland's father, Henry Holland senior, began an association with Lancelot 'Capability' Brown in the mid 1700s and this proved to be of considerable benefit to Holland the younger, who developed skills as a designer, no doubt gaining experience through speculative developments in London. Henry Holland senior worked closely with Lancelot Brown at Ashridge in Hertfordshire in the early 1760s, and Brown's reputation and connections must have opened many doors to the able and ambitious son. Indeed in 1777 the Park at Southill was redesigned by 'Capability' Brown for Viscount Torrington. In 1773 Henry Holland married Brown's daughter Bridget by which time he had established his own thriving architectural practice employing, among others, John Soane who was to become one of the most creative and original architects of his time.

The commission at Southill came relatively late in Holland's busy and successful career. Unlike many of his contemporaries Holland had not travelled to the Mediterranean and perhaps this apparent privation allowed Holland to develop such an individual style which was to influence both his contemporaries and his successors. Samuel Whitbread I had purchased the Southill estate in 1795 and immediately began to plan the extensive alterations which took four years to complete. In 1796 Samuel Whitbread I died and was succeeded by his son Samuel

Samuel Whitbread II by John Opie, 1804

Whitbread II, and a long and surprisingly close relationship developed between the new patron and his architect.

Admiral George Byng, first Viscount Torrington, created a new mansion on the site of the present house, and set out the park and gardens at a cost which apparently strained his considerable fortune. Documentary evidence indicates that Torrington's house was almost certainly completed by November 1726. Almost seventy years later, by which time the family fortune had completely disappeared, Torrington's grandson, John Byng the diarist, lamented the late Admiral's extravagance. Following a visit to Turvey near Bedford in 1793, where John Higgins was building Turvey House on a bare hillside, Byng wrote "Now this is so like a London tradesman, or an admiral! My grandfather thus built Southill House in an open field; and had to plant trees, to dig canals, to make mounts, and to throw away his money in vile taste! When ready-built houses, and ready-grown trees are to be bought all at once. . . as wise people have done, purchasing house, furniture, and wine all at a stroke; and sit themselves down, the next day, in their own houses, quietly with all their comforts and luxuries about them. Men do not make fortunes before they are 50 years of age, when they are harass'd and worn out; and then should buy a place ready cut and dry'd. Now my grandfather admiral and my uncle admiral would, from folly and pride, rear places, and they both died ere they were finish'd, leaving their heirs encumber'd with great houses and inadequate estates".

A view of Southill House by Badeslade about the year 1739, published in *Vitruvius Brittanicus*, shows the house and park. The Palladian style house has a southerly approach with a formal park extending to the north, with vast avenues of trees, woodland and water gardens, and formal ponds and canals to the north west. In the distance, floating serenely at the further extremity of the canal, is a three masted man'o'war, no doubt artistic licence to flatter the Admiral!

There is no documentary or other evidence yet found to suggest an architect. The Palladian style of Torrington's new house prompted the suggestion that Isaac Ware may have been the architect, although it is now known that the date of the house is too early for any possible connection. Ware only started his apprenticeship in 1721 and his first known commission came in 1733 in London. Without firm evidence of the date of Torrington's house a connection with Ware was perhaps a reasonable assumption. Ware was a strict follower of the Palladian ideal which was the stylistic inspiration for the new house. Ware's patron, the third Earl of Burlington (1694-1753), was enormously influential in the establishment of the Palladian revival in England during the early Georgian period. The originator of this architectural style was Andrea Palladio (1508-1580) who studied ancient classical architecture in Italy and established a set of principles embodied in his famous publication *The Four Books of Architecture*. This work was translated by Isaac Ware from the Italian and re-published in 1738 under the patronage of Lord Burlington. A later link with Ware is more possible. Ware worked extensively in the 1740s at nearby Chicksands Priory, seat of Sir Danvers Osborn, Lord Torrington's grandson, and he may then have supervised some minor alterations at Southill. Henry Holland's plan drawings of the house as it was in 1795 compared to earlier plan drawings show changes to the Eating Room and Drawing Room and perhaps this was the work of Isaac Ware.

No other candidate as architect of this house has been suggested in place of Ware. It could be that the Admiral, a practical man, built the house without an architect, employing an experienced builder to provide a degree of competence.

Drawings survive in the Southill archive to give a good understanding of the house built by Lord Torrington. The design was typically Palladian in style consisting of a three bay, five storey main block flanked by two three-storey wings. The pedimented pavilions are dominated by large Venetian windows facing north and south. Single storey arcaded links join the pavilions to the main block. The house was brick faced as illustrated in coloured versions of the elevational drawings. During the recent restoration work, red facing bricks with mortar joints lined out in the early eighteenth century style were found behind the 1796 stone ashlar facing. Indeed, much evidence of the first house survives, mostly hidden, except in the basement and attic where doors, doorcases and oak floorboards have remained in rooms considered by Holland to have been architecturally unimportant.

If we compare it with the present house, the plan layout of Lord Torrington's house could hardly have been more different. The principal entrance was to the south by way of a single storey pedimented portico, no doubt bearing the family crest. The kitchen lay at the east end of the house in the pavilion. Keeping food warm *en route* to the Eating Room at the other end of the building must have presented considerable practical problems. All the principal rooms at ground floor level faced north, over the park. While this is contrary to modern, and indeed late Georgian, taste there are advantages. Rooms are not brightly lit by sunlight and views over the park are consequently clearer. However slight these advantages may seem it is quite apparent that the layout of the rooms did not please a tenant of the house, Lord Polwarth, who wrote in 1779 that Southill was "a place built and fitted up by an Ideot, with great expence, in which every room and every office is good in itself, but every room and every office stands in the wrong place". However, Polwarth's wife considered that there were sufficient good rooms in the centre block for them to make themselves comfortable. "Most of the servants then lay in the underground floor, but there are 3 or 4 rooms near the kitchen that would do for our upper servants at least."

The early Georgian fashion for red brick, particularly where good building stone was unavailable, fell out of favour in the latter half of the eighteenth century. 'Capability' Brown expressed a particular dislike for red brick facings which in his opinion "could set a valley in a fever". In 1795 Samuel Whitbread I saw that his son would need a seat in Bedfordshire and purchased the Southill estate. There was little delay in appointing Holland to oversee alterations to the house, although the elder Samuel did not live to see the new house occupied. In 1796, following his father's death, Samuel Whitbread II took up the reins and there followed a long and affectionate relationship between the new owner and

The Rebuilding of Southill in 1797 by George Garrard

the architect. Holland transformed the house. A new service wing to the east provided accommodation for the kitchen and laundry. The former Great Hall was extended to the south to become the new Drawing Room. The whole composition was radically recast with a new driveway providing access to the north side of the house. Gone was the grand entrance portico of Torrington's house. The north door into Holland's new Hall was a wonderful understatement with no architectural emphasis. This severe design was apparently not appreciated by a later generation, who built a new Hall and *Porte Cochère* at the west end of the house. To the south, colonnaded loggias softened the formal relationship between the house and garden. A contemporary picture by Garrard shows the house in the process of rebuilding. Masons are seen working huge blocks of stone refacing the house. Interestingly, Holland chose the only available local stone for the rebuilding. Quarried from the harder chalk beds, Totternhoe clunch is a relatively weak stone and therefore perhaps a surprising choice. This deficiency must have been known to Holland and the more durable Portland stone was used for the cornice, with Ketton stone for the parapets. The clunch facings have not weathered well, and recent repair work included substantial refacing, again using clunch from the nearby Totternhoe quarry. Previously, refacing had been carried out

Henry Holland, bust by George Garrard

using Portland stone and Bath stone with disastrous visual effect. The warm honey colour of weathered clunch is its great attraction and this, too, must have been known to Holland.

The masterpiece created by Holland was a great delight to his patron. The beauty and subtlety of this wonderful house have been widely acclaimed and the house considered Holland's masterpiece. Decorated and partly furnished by

Holland, Southill House provides a unique combination of formal grandeur and domestic warmth and simplicity which has been enjoyed by succeeding generations of the family for two hundred years.

Holland died in 1806 soon after completion of the new house. As a mark of affection Whitbread commissioned a bust of Holland which bears the following inscription on the plinth:

> "Business is often friendship's end
> From business once there rose a Friend.
> Holland! that Friend I found in thee,
> Thy loss I feel, when e'er I see
> The labours of thy polished mind:
> Thy loss I feel, when e'er I find
> The comforts of this happy place;
> Thy loss I feel when e'er I trace
> In house, in garden, or in ground,
> The scene of every social round.
> Farewell !
> In life I honoured thee;
> In death thy name respected be".

Samuel Whitbread II encouraged many contemporary artists including George Garrard and Garrard's father-in-law, Sawrey Gilpin. Pictures and sculptures by Garrard survive together with painted overdoors by Gilpin. The French artist, Alexandre Louis Delabrière painted the superb decoration in the Painted Parlour which survives to this day, together with excellent contemporary painted decoration in the Dining Room which has recently been skilfully restored. The whole composition is a remarkable combination of patron and artist, producing a great work of architecture with pictures and furnishings which have survived changing fashions over a period of two centuries, and Southill remains essentially an elegant and comfortable family home.

Chapter 4

The Estate and the Enclosure Movement

by NORMAN PARRY

WITH THE PURCHASE of the Southill and Potton estates in 1795 from the fourth Viscount Torrington, Samuel Whitbread I completed his major acquisitions in Bedfordshire. On his death in the following year his son Samuel Whitbread II inherited about 12,300 acres of which 10,500 were in Bedfordshire, mainly in Cardington, Southill and Old Warden. His total rent roll in 1797 was just short of £22,000 of which 54% came from Bedfordshire properties.

During the nineteen years that Samuel Whitbread II was in possession of the Southill Estate, he concentrated on building it up in the Southill and Cardington area by careful purchases, and by disposing of outlying holdings in Bedfordshire and in other counties. By 1808, of the out of county lands, only a few acres in Hertfordshire and Dorset remained besides the 354 acres in Essex and the London properties. The rest was all within Bedfordshire. During this period he bought about 2,200 acres, and sales of unwanted land gave a net gain of around 1,400 acres. By 1815 his local estate totalled about 12,000 acres, an increase of 15% on his 1796 inheritance. Having made the last major purchase of his life in 1815 he was able to say: "I have at length completed and paid for a large purchase of land immediately adjoining to my Southill property . . . ..[a] purchase much desired by my Father as interrupting his Cardington property, making all together the most entire possession which is anywhere to be met with for its extent".

Samuel was not completely successful in selling off the unwanted parts of his Bedfordshire estate. Preparations were made in 1813 for selling the Potton property including the market tolls, the rights appertaining to the lordships of the four manors, and 594 acres of land, but no buyer could be found, and so Potton remained part of the Southill estate until 1917. The catalogue printed for the proposed sale described the property as having the land tax redeemed, as this added to the value.

The question of increased productivity and value very much occupied the minds of many of the country's major landowners, although Samuel Whitbread II often appears to have regarded agriculture as a hobby, the brewery as a source of income and politics as his business. Despite this he kept in touch with developments in farming techniques, particularly those popularised at the agricultural meetings at Holkham and Woburn. One of his interests was Merino sheep, and the quality of the wool and mutton produced by them. In one of his letters he mentions that William Hale was sending 50 Southdown ewes to Samuel's Spanish ram. Other letters mention Devon cattle travelling to Holkham in Norfolk by way of Southill, and a proposed trial of Ayrshire cattle. There are also references to co-operation with the Duke of Bedford in projects including the setting up of the Bedfordshire Show and Agricultural Society.

The day to day running of the Southill Estate was in the hands of James Lilburne, a former Cardington schoolmaster, and his son Thomas, whose education had been paid for by Whitbread. Both took a very active part in the changes which took place as a result of the enclosure movement in the parishes where the Whitbreads held land. There had been considerable concern in the latter half of the eighteenth century as to the country's ability to feed its rapidly increasing population. An estimated population increase of 43% in England between 1750 and 1800 and a series of poor harvests in the 1790s led to calls for more enclosures of the open fields in order to set up more efficient farming systems and so increase the production of grain. The official fears were justified when the population more than doubled in the fifty years after 1801.

What is meant by the term enclosure? W E Tate described the pre-enclosure system as the time when "the holdings of each proprietor or occupier were widely scattered in small plots in each field and appended to them was the use of common meadow and common pasture; arable, meadow and pasture alike being subject to some degree of communal control and management", and Tate talks of the enclosure as "The replacement of these holdings by individual hedged or fenced closes and farms and the replacement of communal control by that of persons pursuing policies of enlightened self-interest". In a Bedfordshire unenclosed village the common arable land was in three or more enormous fields, and the individual farmer or husbandman had scattered unfenced strips in each of them, the land in each field being subject to a customary rotation of crops: often one year wheat, the next year barley and the third year fallow, the fallow field being pasture for the community's sheep and cows, as were the other two fields after harvest. In addition a man would have strips in the common meadows for hay, and after the hay had been carried these too were open for common pasturage. According to his acreage of arable, each man had the right to put so many cows or sheep on the common pastures. Any area of infertile waste ground could be used by any inhabitant for grazing. The owners of some ancient cottages had the right to put some sheep or cows on the common pastures though they had no arable. Such a right had gone with the cottage from antiquity, and explains the occurrence of such rules as the one of 1618 stating "no new erected cottage shall have any benefit on the commons".

Many villagers abandoned the life of a peasant farmer for that of a craftsman or tradesman, and the attractions of expanding towns drew others away from their place of birth, and often the land left became the target of those eager to increase their holdings of strips scattered thoughout the open arable fields. The desire to bring these dispersed holdings together into a compact farm free from the old restrictions, and so far more productive and profitable, was the reason for the landowners' interest in enclosure, as long as the cost of the process did not take too much out of their pockets. James Lilburne, Whitbread's agent, writing prior to the enclosure of Cardington, lists the advantages as "laying the arable land of each farm as nearly as may be to the homesteads and by discharging it from the right of Common and the obligation to keep it in particular seasons, to admit of an improved course of cultivation. As to the meadow, instead of the minute and inconvenient divisions in which it now lies, to allot the share of each proprietor in one piece and to give him the entire right of that which he now has in severalty only from Lady Day to Lammas. And by draining. To these improvements will be added the increased value of the commons and waste lands by allotting to each proprietor his share. The arable land if allotted in the manner proposed will not require more than two thirds of the horses now necessary. There will be a considerable saving in labour, the value of the crops will be increased and more stock may be kept. The tenants can afford to pay after the allotments at least the following rents: Arable per acre 15s (75p) and meadow 27s 6d (£1.37)" The pre-enclosure rents quoted were 11s 6d (57p) and 22s 6d (£1.12).

A further note in the Cardington preliminaries states "It is not proposed to discharge the land from tithes, because if that were done, a great proportion of the best land would go for the tithe allotment". The payment of tithes in kind was a contentious subject, particularly among nonconformists, and the opportunity was sometimes taken to combine the enclosure of the open field land with the abolition of tithes by making instead an allotment of land to the tithe owners. Of the

Whitbread parishes, Potton was the only one where the two actions took place simultaneously. Apparently neither Samuel Whitbread II nor his son William Henry (who succeeded him) had any objections, perhaps because their estate was in the part which had been enclosed in 1775, and was not much affected by the large allocation of land to the incumbent and to the Thaxted Charities (who owned the great tithes). In other parishes a separate tithe commutation award compensated the tithe owners with a set money charge on each field, rather than as previously in actual produce. The tithe award for Elstow is dated December 1850.

The Government saw that there was a need to increase the supply of food and it was agreed that the compact farms which were the result of an enclosure would do just that. Therefore measures were introduced to facilitate the passage through parliament of enclosure acts, one of which was needed for each parish where the land was in the hands of more than one owner.

The enclosures of parishes in which the estate of Samuel Whitbread II was involved were Southill 1797; Bedford St Mary 1799; Elstow 1800; Cardington and Shillington 1802; Wilstead 1809; and Potton (partially enclosed in 1775) in 1814, but with a delay until 1832 before the award was completed. Delays in other places were shorter. The award procedure had by this time been standardised and with a few minor variations enclosures follow the same pattern. Briefly, commissioners appointed under the particular enclosure act would take over the running of the parish common fields until such time as an accurate survey had been carried out of all those who held land or rights of common under the old system, with the value and extent of each property. The available land, both arable and meadow and common pasture, would then be shared between those entitled, in such proportions as the commissioners decided was appropriate. In addition the road system was as far as possible rationalised, to reduce the length and so the cost of highway maintenance, and necessary public drains were laid out, and the responsibility of owners for the upkeep of hedges and ditches or other boundaries decided. All of this would be incorporated into the final award text. Many of these awards and their accompanying maps are still used to settle disputes regarding rights of way and boundaries. Survival of documents relating to the work of the enclosure commissioners is variable. The final award with its map has usually survived, but the details of the preliminary work of the commissioners and their surveyor has often been lost. Of the parishes mentioned above commissioners' papers for the Cardington and Potton enclosures have survived and give a fairly accurate picture of events, and it is reasonable to assume that what happened in the other parishes would have been much the same.

In Southill the four gentlemen noted as commissioners were George Maxwell

Cartouche from the Henlow Enclosure Award Map, 1798
One of the figures is said to be George Maxwell, a commissioner for the Southill Enclosure

of Spalding, James Ellis, Edward Platt of Lidlington and Thomas Thorpe of Great Barford. One of these was also the surveyor, possibly Maxwell, who is reputed to be depicted in the picture of enclosure work being done in the fields of Henlow. In Bedford St Mary, those concerned were Robert Edwards of Boughton in Northants., James Lilburne of Cardington and Southill (agent for Samuel Whitbread) and Thomas Stone of Grays Inn, Middlesex. Stone was probably the author of the survey of the agriculture of the county of 1794, one of the publications which was much in favour of the enclosure movement. The surveyor was Charles Bloodworth of Kimbolton. In Wilstead and Elstow Lilburne appears to have acted alone, and the Elstow act states that a surveyor was not required because an existing plan could be used. The list of commissioners in the Shillington act illustrates one of the problems which could occur. The original three were Joseph Eade, Thomas Thorpe and Joseph Truelove. Eade, a Hitchin solicitor in the practice which handled the Whitbread family affairs, refused to act, and was replaced by Joseph Pawsey. He resigned in 1807 and was replaced by John Maugham. Thorpe died in 1813 and his place was taken by Thomas Brown. Truelove resigned in 1816 and was replaced by Alexander Watford. The award was finally signed in 1821, nineteen years after work began.

In Potton, the last of the acts to be considered here, there was some disagreement about the appointment of the commissioners, but eventually three were nominated. Thomas Brown represented Whitbread, John Burcham the tithe owners, and Charles Bloodworth the other proprietors. The solicitor employed to put the act through parliament was Robert Lindsell of Biggleswade, and another local lawyer, George Pedley, was appointed clerk to the commissioners. The surveyor for this enclosure was Thomas Lilburne, the son of James. From the above lists you can see that certain men were involved in a number of enclosures, being considered experts in the work, but this might have contributed to delays in the completion of the final awards. There were a number of changes during the eighteen years it took to complete the Potton enclosure. Brown died before taking any part and was replaced by James Lilburne, who had also been nominated as one of the clerks. He died and was replaced by William Jones and in 1826 Bloodworth died and his place was taken by William Wells Gardner.

In the preliminary discussions for the Cardington act it was proposed that James Lilburne should be the commissioner, but as a letter from the Whitbreads' solicitor Wilshere pointed out, he was barred from doing so. "One commissioner has been preferred in this as in several other cases with us to lessen the expense and to expedite the business, two purposes which I have found much better answered by one than more. . . . . . Mr Eade is a professional man at Hitchin, generally approved. Mr Lilburne was the commissioner thought of but being an agent of some of the proprietors, a late standing order of the House of Commons excluded him; he is however proposed to be the surveyor, and the execution of the business will rest very much on him". The letter is dated 4 May 1802. Eade was named in the act passed the following month but he refused to act, and at a meeting held on 30 July Samuel Whitbread and Thomas Morgan, as land owners, chose Lilburne to take Eade's place, a way round the parliamentary prohibition which kept within the law. The desire on the part of the land owners to keep costs to a minimum can be understood when we discover that Whitbread's share of the Cardington expenses came to £1842 8s 2d (£1842.41), nearly 64% of the total. Much of the cost went on administration, for example the commissioners were paid for their attendance and for travelling time both before and after each meeting. By the time of the later enclosures on our list this was in the region of six guineas a day. George Maxwell acted in at least a hundred enclosures, many of them simultaneously, and John Burcham, who acted for the tithe owners in Potton, is known to have done the same in at least sixty nine others. Tate commented that "the actual work of enclosure might be a very profitable business for those taking part in it regularly. The most glaring example appears to be John Burcham ... He is known to have acted in at least sixty-nine enclosures between 1801 and 1840 .... He died in 1841 leaving a fortune of about £600,000. Russell [the author from whom Tate is quoting] is not being unduly cynical when he says that, although he does not allege that the whole of Burcham's fortune came from enclosure, it would certainly be surprising if after acting in sixty-nine enclosures John Burcham had not died a rich man".

The Lilburnes, father and son, who were Samuel Whitbread II's very able estate agents, were on a fixed salary. £450 is quoted as their joint income in 1801, £500 in 1803 rising to £800 in 1814. Out of this James paid Thomas what he thought proper, which in 1803 was £127. In one letter Thomas says that because of an increase in his family he could not exist on what his father was allowing him, and he wanted 200 guineas.

Whether the tenants were content is not stated. Certainly eight were given notice to quit immediately prior to the Cardington enclosure, possibly because their holdings would disappear in the reallocation of land. A somewhat cavalier attitude appears in a letter of September 1813 from James Lilburne to Whitbread. He suggested that the rent for Bury Farm in Southill, then £230, should be £530. He goes on to say that the church rate for the period was £778 14s, and that it was impossible for this to be paid in addition to the suggested advance. As the church rate was so disliked he suggested that Samuel Whitbread should take over the payment of the church rate himself, as this would be popular with his tenants, and objections from them to rent increases would be less likely.

Five months later Lilburne wrote that he had managed to increase rents without too many complaints from the tenants. "We had a moderate degree of grumbling from N.... but Mr. J.... is an infant in discontent and conversation when compared with P.... All the rest of the tenants quiet". A document of 1815 gives figures of acreage, rents and sums spent on improvements for four farms in Southill:

	Acreage	Rent	Improvements
New Rowney	502a 2r 0p	£454	£950
Old Rowney	449a 2r 7p	£542	£1900
Pains	374a 1r 35p	£690	£2000
Bodgers	356a 3r 32p	£804	£1750

It is noticeable that there was a large variation in rents between farms, the ones above ranging from 18s (90p) to 45s (£2.25) per acre, and this could be related to the fertility of the soil of that particular farm or to the cost of the improvements. In Potton twelve years later a similar situation existed. The three main farms brought in £1 0s 3d (£1.1); £1 4s (£1.20) and £1 12s 6d (£1.62) per acre, and the rents on the smaller holdings ranged from 19s (90p) to 45s (£2.25) per acre. Here the situation had probably improved considerably from that of November 1814 when Lilburne wrote that of the eleven fields totalling 121 acres, he had managed to let ten to produce the former rents but "the poor gardeners by the low prices of their vegetables are very much distressed and have no inclination to take land as they have done before. I am fearful from what I know that more of the land will be given up".

The early years of the nineteenth century were a time of change in the agriculture of the county. The enclosure movement brought to an end a way of life of the labourer or small farmer not too dissimilar from that of his medieval predecessors. At the same time the influx of money from trade brought improvements in estates and in the transport system. The improvements were accompanied by rent increases but the Whitbread tenants were probably more fortunate than those elsewhere. The increase in the gross rental from the Bedfordshire estates was roughly 48% over the period from 1797 to 1813. The quoted rises in other areas range from 70% to as high as 90%. It may be that Samuel Whitbread II considered it politically expedient to limit the rises, perhaps foreseeing the problems that would arise at the end of the Napoleonic Wars. It has not been possible to continue to look at the farming situation in the later years of the last century in the same detail. A few documents have survived, but not in suffient quantity to provide a balanced and comprehensive story.

Chapter 5

Southill – A Sporting Estate

FIELD SPORTS by SAM WHITBREAD

SPORT AND THE English countryside have always gone hand in hand. For some it has meant recreation, for some a source of income, and some have depended on what others call sport for food. Whatever one's view of field sports there is no denying their influence on the English landscape – so many of the woods, spinneys and hedges we see round us today would not be there but for the sport they have provided over the centuries.

But although it is shooting and hunting that have shaped so much of the Bedfordshire countryside, other more popular sports have taken place on the Southill Estate for the past two hundred years. Cricket is covered elsewhere in this chapter, but archery, horseracing, football, tennis and even skating have at various times taken place on the estate.

Archery became a welcome feature of nineteenth century country house life, largely because ladies, debarred from almost all other sports, could take part. It is said that archery competitions took place on what is now the cricket field in Southill Park.

Horse racing was a regular part of the county's social life. First held in 1730 on Cow Meadow, west of Elstow, on the edge of what was to become the Southill Estate, Bedford Races were an occasion for dressing up in one's finery, meeting one's neighbours, attending an Assembly at Bedford and drinking freely. Racing continued on Cow Meadow up to the 1870s.

The fortunes of village football have risen and fallen over the years but teams at Southill, Cardington, Elstow and Cotton End have thrived at different times on village playing fields provided by the estate. At Southill a Lawn Tennis Club has been a feature of village life since the 1950s.

Skating may seem a surprising addition to the list of sporting activities on the estate, but certainly in the 1890s the ice on the Round Basin and the Lake was "thick enough for skaters from the village" and for an ice hockey match. The writer well remembers the hard winter of 1942 when not only skating took place on the frozen lake in the park. The Army, then in occupation of part of Southill House and park, arranged a series of highly-precarious motor cycle races on the ice around the island.

Southill Lake has also been famed for its coarse fishing. In 1819 it yielded a pike weighing $32^1/_2$ lbs, but in about 1900 two pike of 52 lbs and 48 lbs were found stranded in the mud after one of the sluices broke and the water level suddenly fell. In recent years, quantities of tench, bream and roach, as well as pike, have been caught. At one time this century Samuel Howard Whitbread decided to introduce trout into the lake, which was completely drained so that the coarse fish could be removed. Unfortunately, some of the pike must have been overlooked, probably lurking in the mud, so that the trout soon disappeared.

Hunting

Hunting with hounds has existed in England from the earliest times. At the beginning of the eighteenth century hares and foxes were hunted with the same packs of hounds, though in Bedfordshire the Orlebars bred foxhounds at Hinwick, and there was also a pack kept at Wrest Park.

Towards the end of the eighteenth century, the Duke of Bedford had established three hound kennels at Woburn, Eaton Socon and Oakley, and it was probably hunting that drew Sam Whitbread II to Bedfordshire from his first home, Woolmers in Hertfordshire. In 1789 Sam's father wrote to John Howard from Bedwell, his own Hertfordshire home, "my son is near me at present but moving soon to Cardington and other places for Hunting".

At the same time as Sam Whitbread II was rebuilding the house at Southill, concern about war with Napoleon and the resulting tax increases led the Duke of Bedford and William Lee Antonie (who had recently changed his Colworth hare hounds to foxhounds) to convert what had been their private hunts into a subscription hunt, with Antonie as Master and the Duke, Antonie and Whitbread as the main subscribers. Thus the Oakley Hunt was born in 1798.

Although most of the Southill Estate lay outside the Oakley country, Sam Whitbread II and later his two sons, William Henry and Samuel Charles, hunted regularly with the Oakley. Sam II himself gave up hunting in 1807: the considerable expense (the annual subscription of £750 is the equivalent of about £17,000 today), his wife's dislike of the sport, and the burdens of his Parliamentary and Bedfordshire activities all combined to persuade him to abandon the hunting field. All the same, he admitted being unable to withdraw "without a heavy heart. I look back upon our joyous morning meetings with great regret". Occasionally, in the years to come, he would be tempted to return to the sport he loved so much. A year after leaving the Oakley, he writes that he has "returned from hunting with Mr Dunn's hounds ... a most brilliant burst of 50 minutes over the Cambridgeshire country, but we lost our fox". In December 1810 he is writing to his friend Antonie "I miss the chase exceedingly. The want of it takes the zest of Southill at this time of year".

After the death of Samuel Whitbread II in 1815, his sons William Henry and Samuel Charles continued the family link with the Oakley hunt. In 1830 a row blew up between members of the Oakley Club and the Master, Grantley Berkeley, whom they accused of not hunting the Oakley country efficiently. They recommended that Berkeley engage a huntsman for the remaining two years of his term. When he refused, they threatened to withdraw their subscriptions and later recommended that he resign as Master. Acrimonious correspondence between Samuel Charles and Berkeley led to a challenge to a duel. Both parties duly assembled at the Swan Inn in Bedford, but a last-minute withdrawal by Berkeley ensured that no blood was shed.

On his eightieth birthday in 1876 Samuel Charles Whitbread sat down ".. to put on record some events which I witnessed with the Oakley hounds. My father was a perfect horseman and took pains to teach me". Samuel Charles had evidently kept a hunting journal as he describes in detail what he calls "the greatest run" he had enjoyed with the Oakley, when on 11 February 1815 hounds met at Colworth, found in Odell Wood and ran four hours and 36 miles before killing the fox at Rothwell near Market Harborough. Only the Whitbread brothers, Lord Tavistock and seven others were "in at the death", and they had to leave their exhausted horses at Market Harborough and ride home on post horses.

But we must not assume that fox hunting in Bedfordshire in the nineteenth century was the prerogative of the gentry, any more than it is today. Henry John Peacock was a tenant farmer on the Southill Estate at Wilstead. It was said by one of his descendants that he "lived his life on horseback and horses meant as much to him as people". Peacock admitted that his was "not a bad life. I hunted five days a week, went to market on the sixth and to church on the seventh – that was my week". When asked how he managed to run his farm, he replied "Well, the foreman would throw gravel at my window at 6 o'clock and I'd give him the orders for the day".

Although members of the Whitbread family have always remained loyal to the Oakley – they have held unbroken membership of the Oakley Club from its foundation in 1814 to the present day – much of the Southill Estate has traditionally been hunted by the Cambridgeshire and Hertfordshire hunts.

The Cambridgeshire hounds were established in 1827. Unlike the Oakley, which had at the centre of its country a sizeable town, Bedford, the Cambridgeshire had the disadvantage of Cambridge being in a corner of its territory. *British Hunts and Huntsmen*, published in 1909, states that the real centre "is Biggleswade, which has been the home of so many good sportsmen". Among these was Jack Race, who also hunted with the Oakley. During Grantley Berkeley's mastership of the Oakley, Jack Race one day "got away . . . rather too soon" (that is, in front of the Master). Berkeley promptly swore at him. "I didn't come out to be damned", complained Race. "Then go home and be damned" retorted Berkeley.

The woods on the Southill Estate seemed to provide equally good sport for shooting and for hunting in the nineteenth century. An 1850 map of the Cambridgeshire country lists Southill among places where hounds met. The Warden Woods were described as being "spacious and useful" and, together with Sheerhatch Wood at Northill and Chicksands Wood, were described as "one of the best bits of woodland country in England".

But Southill has perhaps suffered through being on the edge of three hunts, the Oakley, the Cambridgeshire and the Hertfordshire, all of whom, at various times, have laid claim to its thousand acres of woodland. When the Hertfordshire surrendered the northern part of its country to become the Vale of Aylesbury in 1970, the Cambridgeshire stepped in, but in the last few years the Oakley has extended its territory to include the estate.

Hares also were hunted. The Biggleswade Harriers were founded in 1811 and William Henry Whitbread's stepson, Turner Macan, kept a pack of harriers at Elstow from 1852 to 1864. A most unusual quarry for Southill was a white stag which in 1847 was described by George Race (son of the Jack who was 'damned' by Grantley Berkeley while out with the Oakley) in his *Seventy Years a Master*, as the "biggest animal I ever hunted". Found in Four Acres, the stag ran through Rowney Warren, Chicksands, Wrest, Barton, Pulloxhill, Toddington and Hockliffe – seventeen miles without a check. Here he was bayed by hounds before taking off again. But, as Race says, "my horse was then quite done", and he had to take his hounds home, reaching Biggleswade as the church clock struck midnight. The stag was captured alive at Leighton Buzzard. It had come from Woburn, but as a mark of respect to the big-hearted beast, the Duchess of Bedford presented it to Queen Victoria at Windsor.

Shooting

Shooting, whether for food or for sport, was part of the English way of life long before Samuel Whitbread I bought the Southill Estate. The previous owners, the

Southill keepers in the 1930's
George Hill, Bob Hill, Herbert Linford and George Edwards

Byng family, preserved game at Southill, and when the Viscount Torrington commissioned the artist George Stubbs to paint some scenes on his Bedfordshire estate, one of these depicted game-keepers.

The relationship between farming, shooting and the landscape has been evolving for well over 200 years. Just as the enclosures provided the impetus for a revolution in farming and stock breeding, so the planting of hedges had a highly beneficial effect on game shooting (as well as on hunting). What had previously been uncultivated scrub and woodland and vast tracts of arable gave way to a patchwork of fields and hedges which many of us remember from our childhood. What is often forgotten is that to some the partition of open countryside by the enclosures appeared to be nothing more than "the destruction of beautiful wild scenery". Landowners who preserved game knew the value of hedges, spinneys and warm woods for providing what we would today call the ideal habitat for game birds, and it has been said that "as much of our lovely countryside was created by sporting landowners because of the gun, as had earlier been created by the axe or the plough".

At Southill, the pheasant, the partridge and the hare were the main quarry, although quantities of rabbits were taken not only for food but to protect growing crops of corn or grass. In the eighteenth century birds were mainly shot as they perched in the trees or on the ground. However, the year 1770 saw the publication of a book called *The Art of Shooting Flying*. By 1800 shooting perching had given way to shooting flying, and in 1807 we are told that it was "not exactly at present the custom for Gentlemen to shoot on the ground".

For the first twenty years of the nineteenth century, farming in England was dominated by the Napoleonic Wars and grain farming was profitable. The earliest shooting records on the Southill Estate are from 1811, when between ten and fifteen brace of partridges would be shot on days on September stubbles at Cardington or Wilstead. These are probably the personal records of Sam Whitbread II as the entries are discontinued after the 1814 season – he died in July 1815.

Between 1820 and 1850 farming declined as Europe opened up to free trade. Grain prices fell and food prices with them. A shift to grassland meant that landlords had to look at other means of generating income from their estates and shooting rents offered an alternative. This period saw the development of the sporting potential of the Southill Estate with trees being planted and existing woodlands being carefully managed. The art of driven shooting and the development of safer and faster-shooting guns led to a greater interest in covert shooting and the rearing of pheasants.

By 1820 William Henry had succeeded his father as the Squire of Southill. His game book shows that in that year a total of 346 pheasants, 719 partridges and 358 hares were accounted for. In September alone he was out on thirteen days, sometimes in the company of his brother, Samuel Charles, and one or two others. The game would have been 'walked-up', but bags of up to 25 brace of partridges show how plentiful they were at that time.

The partridge of the Bedfordshire stubble fields was, of course, the grey or common partridge (*Perdix perdix*). The Red-Leg or French partridge (*Alectoris rufa*) began to be introduced into England in the 1790s. The bird's first appearance in Bedfordshire was at Wilden in 1845 and it was described as being common in the Luton area by 1855. At about this time, partridge driving began to take the place of walking-up. First introduced in Suffolk in 1845, driving involved a team of 'bush beaters' flushing the birds from the stubbles and hedges and driving them towards a line of guns concealed behind a hedge. This led to larger teams of sportsmen in the field (up to 10) and of course to employment opportunities for the beaters.

Pheasants were also driven in this way and the game book for the 1864/5 season records a day in January when 270 pheasants were shot by a team of ten guns. Partridges still occupied the attention of sportsmen in the early part of the season and in September 1864 there are records of no fewer than twenty five days' shooting, with 550 brace of partridges being accounted for.

By now pheasants were beginning to be reared on the estate with eggs being collected from wild nests and put under broody hens or bantams, thus encouraging the wild pheasants to lay again. During the 1860s, the game book shows a steady rise in the total number of pheasants shot until in 1870/1 for the first time the total number of pheasants recorded exceeds that of partridges.

The late 1870s saw a series of bad harvests and the beginning of imports of meat and grain from the Americas and Australasia. Farming fortunes declined once more. Farms were hard to let in spite of annual rent remissions. Much land was left fallow and not farmed and once again landlords recognized the value of shooting rents, and that unfarmed land yielded good sport both for shooting and hunting.

At this time the shooting at Elstow and Cardington appears to have been let, the tenant of Cardington being General Mills, whose wife Gertrude was the daughter of Samuel Charles Whitbread. The Cardington beat produced partridges and a few hares. The main pheasant beats on the estate were the Park, Keepers' Warren, Exeter Wood, and Warden Great and Little Woods, whilst partridges were also shot at Broom, Stanford and Rowney.

Between 1880 and the first World War shooting (and particularly pheasant shooting) took on a new significance for country estates. Landowners vied with each other for the prize of luring the Prince of Wales (later King Edward VII) to their shoots with promises of huge bags of pheasants, extravagant food and drink, and pretty ladies. This obsession with big bags of pheasants reached its rather distasteful climax in 1913, when on 18 December at Hall Barn, Beaconsfield, seven guns, including King George V and the Prince of Wales, accounted for 3,937 pheasants. Returning to London in the train, it is said that the Prince of Wales noticed that the King was unusually silent. At last he turned to the Prince and said quietly "Perhaps we over-did it today".

Happily at Southill things were not done on this scale, although the records show that from 1884 until 1911 there was a steady increase in the total number of pheasants shot each season – in 1884: 1,123; in 1911: 4,317. In 1911, on three consecutive days six guns shot 2,270 pheasants.

This large-scale rearing of pheasants in the years leading up to the Great War attracted the attention of no less a figure than the future Prime Minister himself. Speaking at Bedford in 1913, at the opening of his 'Land Campaign', Lloyd George said "Here is one farmer who was sowing his crop – it was a field of mangels – the man assured me that there was not one mangel out of a dozen that

Southill shooting party on the 80th birthday of Samuel Howard Whitbread, January 1938

was not pecked and destroyed by pheasants, and that was a field that was clear of the plantations. Where you should have got 35 tons here you could not have had more than ten tons. It was not worth the labour and expense of carting". Labourers in the district said that "the pheasants destroyed the produce of their gardens" (*The Times* 15 October 1913). Whether this incident referred to the Southill Estate is not recorded!

During the first World War shooting at Southill continued, albeit on a much-reduced scale. In 1915 the game book records "Samuel Whitbread died on December 25 1915 and shooting ceased for the remainder of the season". He had not himself shot since 1904, by which time his son, Howard, was a regular gun at Southill shoots. Born in 1858, his first recorded day's shooting at Southill was in January 1873 at the age of fifteen, and he continued to shoot regularly up to the age of nearly 82. On his 80th birthday in January 1938, he is recorded as having shot a woodcock – not the easiest of quarry even for a young man. In 1918 Howard was joined in the shooting field by his own son, Simon, who had his first day on 7 January at the age of thirteen, when father and son shot two pheasants in the park.

Things gradually got back to normal again after the Great War and by 1929 – again a time of severe agricultural depression – partridges were flourishing once more, and at Broom and Stanford on consecutive days 168 brace and 149 brace were accounted for. The Second World War saw shooting brought almost to a standstill, and it was not until the 1960s that pheasant bags started to rise significantly again.

But pheasants and partridges were not the only game preserved on the estate. By 1822 over a thousand hares were being killed in a season, and although this figure had dropped to less than half by the 1880s, annual totals of between 200 and 600 were recorded up to the first World War, and up to 300 between the two wars. After World War II, the hare population seems to have fallen dramatically, although numbers increased through the 1960s and 1970s.

In the nineteenth century many hares would have been killed by coursing, and the Game Book for the 1871/2 season records ten days of coursing, mainly at Cardington where a coursing club had been in existence as early as 1836. In that year a presentation was made to William Henry Whitbread "by the Members of the Cardington Coursing Club as a small acknowledgement for the kindness he has so liberally extended to them of sporting over his Manors at Cardington and as a mark of their sincere respect and esteem – April 1836". Other game recorded in the game books are snipe, woodcock and duck, while among the 'various' are included pigeon, moorhen, jay, plover, owl, landrail and 'wild turkey'.

The substantial quantities of game shot in the late nineteenth century lead one to wonder how such numbers were disposed of, and here again the game books provide some answers. At Christmas 1879 49 pheasants and 79 hares were given away to employees and tenants. In Southill village pheasants were distributed to the inn, the butcher, the baker, the vicar, the policeman, two postmen, the blacksmith, the clerk and the wheelwright, while in Shefford recipients included the doctor, the watchmaker and the manager of the gasworks. In 1880 the largesse went even further afield, and the list included the stationmasters at Biggleswade, St Pancras, Euston and Inverness, together with the Superintendent of the Highland Line (from 1858 to 1894 Samuel Whitbread III rented fishing and stalking in Sutherland). In the same year 1880 a total of 683 head of game was given away, 935 sold and 396 went to the house or to the London house.

The game book also records "rabbits used in soup for the poor, three days a week". An eye-witness has described how in the 1890s "on Wednesdays and Saturdays soup was made in the kitchens and there were two big coppers with four or five iron steps up each to reach into them. They would be full of soup and the villagers came up with their cans and Joe Hall, the Odd Man, would say 'How many in the family?' and he would scoop out for each member of the family about a pint of soup . . . and delicious soup it was. It had a lot of yellow split peas in it".

Gamekeepers, of course, played a key role in the provision of sport for successive Southill squires. In 1811 Thomas Delahay complained to Samuel Whitbread II about his treatment. "I have gaint 3/- by your Plase and has laid ought many cold Nights in your Woods and Plantations wen the Rest of your Servants were a Bed and doing so I have decade my Concitution for the Percivation of your Game. I have never had a pleasant word from you in the last three years". Two days later, he followed this up with an apology.

Poaching was commonplace. In some cases where it was simply a matter of 'one for the pot', a justice such as Sam Whitbread II would show leniency, but sometimes vicious armed gangs of poachers would raid the estate, and one such incident is described in the *Annual Register* for 1816. On 9 December 1815 "a gang of notorious and desperate poachers at Biggleswade" set out after dark to shoot pheasants at Southill. Two were armed with guns and the other five with bludgeons. They "agreed to stand by each other and not to be taken". They had shot two pheasants in the Park before attracting the attention of Charles Dines and John Pryer, Head and Underkeeper respectively, and James Gurney, Dines' assistant. The keepers followed the sound of footsteps and shots until they came to a "thick plantation adjoining the Park pales" (Four Acres), where they confronted the gang who at first agreed to leave the Park. However, an argument ensued and Dines told Pryer to get help from George Dilley, the landlord of the White Horse, and his son. As Pryer and the Dilleys returned to the wood a shot rang out and they heard Dines cry out "Lord have mercy upon me; I am a dead man", followed by two more shots. Dines, having been shot in the stomach, had gone down on one knee and fired both barrels of his gun, hitting no fewer than four of the gang, "none materially wounded", in spite of one of them receiving "more than a hundred shots in his back".

Poor Dines died of his wounds the next day and two days later all but two of the gang were arrested and later committed to Bedford Prison. In a melodramatic finale to the tragedy we are told that "as the delinquents were marched off to prison, the bell commenced tolling for the funeral of poor Dines".

William Henry Whitbread placed a memorial stone and planted a yew tree on the spot where Dines fell, and more than fifty years later left in his will £60 to Harriet Button, Dines' daughter.

> CHARLES DINES
> GAMEKEEPER TO THE LATE
> SAMUEL WHITBREAD ESQ.
> WAS BASELY ATTACKED
> ON THIS SPOT BY POACHERS
> 9TH DECEMBER 1815
> AFTER RECEIVING A MORTAL WOUND
> HE FIRED UPON AND WOUNDED
> SEVERAL OF HIS ASSAILANTS
> BUT LIVED NOT
> TO SEE THEM BROUGHT TO JUSTICE
> THIS STONE
> IS PLACED IN REMEMBRANCE
> OF A BRAVE
> AND FAITHFUL SERVANT
> BY W.H. WHITBREAD.

Memorial to Charles Dines, murdered by poachers in 1815

Dogs were another responsibility of the keepers. Pointers had been introduced to England in the early eighteenth century by officers returning from continental battlefields. The 'pointer kennels' in Keepers' Warren (still known as The Kennels to this day) were among the earliest estate buildings at Southill: the plans are dated 1796. Setters and spaniels were used for flushing or 'springing' game from cover. At the beginning of the nineteenth century, the Newfoundland in two varieties – the St Johns and the Labrador – became fashionable, and in 1812 the Southill head keeper, Thomas Delahay, lists sixteen dogs in his kennels: six pointers, five spaniels, two greyhounds, two 'Russians' and a Newfoundland. Jock, the beloved spaniel of Lady Elizabeth Whitbread, has his own memorial on the terrace of Southill House. It is dated 1806 so Jock is clearly exonerated from being the cause of Charles Dines' complaint to Sam Whitbread II in 1813 that he "cannot keep a head of pheasants while the Park is so disturbed".

With the change from walking-up to driving game in the mid-nineteenth century pointers, setters and spaniels became obsolete, and by about 1875 the retriever had become virtually the only dog for the shooting man. It is surprising, therefore, that the first-ever field trial, held on the Southill Estate in 1865, was for pointers and setters.

CRICKET by STEPHEN BUNKER

It was an inauspicious start: opening batsman Edward Payne run out, for a duck, in Southill Park Cricket Club's inaugural fixture against Shefford (at Chicksands) on 27 May 1885. A tentative recovery, led by Samuel Whitbread and Emery King (Southill's wheelwright and undertaker, the son of George King, the local timber merchant), hoisted the total to 95 (7 Southill wickets falling to the Rev G M Osborn) and this proved more than enough against a Shefford side which could only muster 23 and 56, Southill winning by an innings and 16 runs. This was not the first game played at the Park, the Whitbread family having played host at Southill Park to various *ad hoc* games in earlier years. In 1851, for example, a fixture between the County of Bedford and Luton was scheduled to take place

Cricket at Southill, by Thomas Jackson, 1886

at the Park, although in this instance the match did not take place, as the county could not raise a team. At the same time Southill also had its own eleven which played occasional matches against other Bedfordshire villages.

The second fixture (a defeat by Haynes by 55 runs) featured Harold Whitbread (30 not out and 0) and the vicar of Southill, the Rev J C Lambarde (1 and 7). Occasional matches, separate from the club, still continued to be played at Southill Park. In the inaugural season, for example "Mr Whitbread's XI" defeated "Mr T Barnard's XI" with an invitation team which enabled the host to augment his Whitbreads, Kings and Cranfields with that lethal clergyman, the Rev G M Osborn, and also to borrow the fine cricketing schoolmaster, H Coleman, from Haynes.

The club at this stage relied heavily upon the families of Cranfield (farmers from Stanford Bury) and King: these families apart, few players during the 1891 season appear on the census of that year as living in Southill or Stanford. Although in many respects Southill was a self-contained community, lying away from any major line of communication, a feature of the club's history has been its willingness to draw upon players from other villages in eastern Bedfordshire. These included Gerald Gilbert, who kept the village stores at Old Warden and Bob Gale, who hailed from the same village and played for Southill before later joining Middlesex. These augmented other players with closer village connections such as Arthur Swain, the outstanding Captain of the 1950s (when Southill developed a Second XI) who lived at Broom; coalman Harry Bass; White Horse publican Harry Williams; lorry driver Brian Herbert; and Arthur Massey, who initially worked as a gardener on the Southill estate, and who has been the historian of the club. Outstanding was Vic Green, the grandson of an estate carpenter, who made a titanic contribution as a player and an official, and who also used his position in the family building firm for the benefit of the club. The overall trend during the post war era, however, has been for a steady diminution of the proportion of the players who had direct links with Southill and its environs – a feature of English club cricket in general.

Chapter 6

Church and School Life

by JOAN CURRAN

WHEN SAMUEL WHITBREAD I bought Southill House in 1795 to be the seat of the Whitbread family in the county, there was a parish church in each of the villages which formed the main part of the estate – Southill, Cardington and Elstow – and two well supported Independent Meeting Houses, one in Southill dating from about the year 1700, and one in Cardington Cotton End, founded from Bunyan Meeting Bedford in 1776. John Howard had also "caused a cottage at the corner of Harrowden Road [Cardington] to be adapted for religious services". There was a scattering of Sunday schools and small, independently-run day schools in Elstow, Old Warden and Cotton End Cardington, but none of these villages was fortunate enough to have an endowed school established by some past benefactor. In Wilstead, a part of which came within the estate, there was a small school which had been established by an incumbent as far back as 1686, and this had a small endowment.

Over the next hundred years new schools and nonconformist chapels were to appear in all the villages. The nonconformist movements were growing everywhere and in Bedfordshire the number of Methodists, in particular, was steadily increasing. A Methodist chapel seating 115 people, with a house for the minister, was built in Cardington in 1823. The other Methodist chapel in this area (outside the town of Bedford) had been built fifteen years earlier at Wilstead.

The congregations at both Meeting Houses managed to raise the necessary funds for new buildings, Southill at the beginning of the century and Cardington Cotton End in 1836. Both eventually became exclusively Baptist churches, though the one at Cotton End was to alternate between being Congregational and Baptist over the years, at one time admitting people of both persuasions to full membership, as did Bunyan Meeting in Bedford, but finally becoming a Baptist congregation as it is today. Three years after building their own new chapel the Cotton End congregation, together with people from Bunyan Meeting in Bedford, helped the group using the cottage which John Howard had

had adapted for services to establish a meeting house in Cardington. A barn along the Cople Road was rented from Mr Whitbread and converted into a place of worship known as the Union Chapel, which opened in 1839.

The village of Elstow had neither a Methodist nor a Baptist chapel, but a number of people living there were members of Bunyan Meeting at Bedford, and they regularly used the upper floor of the Green House (today called the Moot Hall) for services and Sunday School classes.

Most of the early schools were Sunday Schools belonging to one or other of these churches and chapels, but there were a few day schools. As early as 1782 a number of Cardington children were, as the records say, "At school by Mr. Howard" or "At school by Mr. Whitbread", meaning that one or the other paid a schoolmaster to teach the children. This Mr Whitbread was Samuel I, but twenty years later his son, Samuel Whitbread II, was contributing to three day schools and five Sunday schools within the estate, where between 175 and 200 were receiving some education. The largest day schools were at Cardington, in one of which 18 boys were taught to "Read and Wright", according to Mr Whitbread's agent, and in another 18 girls were taught reading, knitting and needlework. 12 of the boys and 12 of the girls were also "annually cloathed" at a cost of about £27. This village had a variety of small day schools and Sunday schools, reflecting a strong nonconformist influence, which lasted until well into the nineteenth century. The school which overlooks Cardington Green was finally built in 1848 by William Henry Whitbread, with the help of a grant from the British and Foreign Schools Society (a nonconformist organisation), and an extra classroom was added in 1888.

Just a little further along the Southill Road in Cardington, on the opposite side, stood another school set up by the Whitbread family. It was the ladies of the family who were responsible for this and they had had the novel idea of training girls in domestic skills so that they would become better domestic servants and, eventually, housewives. Girls attended this school from the age of seven until they were seventeen, and were instructed in "cooking, washing and all the common work of domestic servants" and farmers were asked to "abstain from offering household employment" to girls under seventeen years of age to allow them to complete their education. It seems to have closed in the early 1890s and is now a private house called Parish Cottage. At Cotton End, the large hamlet within the parish of Cardington, a new board school was built in 1874 to accommodate 140 children, with a house for the master on the same site.

There was no school of any kind in Southill when Samuel Whitbread II came to live in the village but a few years later the Independent Meeting had built their

Southill Lower School, by Bernard West

new meeting house with a schoolroom. Mr Whitbread approached the trustees and asked if he could rent the room for a day school, and his request was agreed to. Mr Joseph Patrick wrote on behalf of the trustees to Mr Whitbread, assuring him that they "cordially approved of his motives" and concluded "Your object, Sir, is such as must meet the approbation of every true Lover of Mankind".

How long the arrangement lasted is not clear, but in 1820 William Henry Whitbread had a new school built in the village. There are accounts for the building for £248, most of which was for the carpenter's work. £40 was received towards this as a grant, but in this case it was from the National Society, a Church of England organisation, and the school was always regarded as a church school. It was a small thatched building which is still in use as part of the school today. An extension was added in 1866, when pupil numbers rose from fifty to nearly a hundred, and in the late 19th century the accommodation was reckoned big enough for over 200 pupils, which must have been a very tight fit indeed. Around the turn of the century infant schools were also built by the Whitbread family in the hamlets of Broom and Stanford.

The children of Elstow were less well catered for than those of the other two villages. In 1818 several children went to school in Bedford "which is one mile distant". Apart from two Sunday schools, one Anglican and one nonconformist, the only other educational establishments for some time seem to have been lace schools and in 1846 a report said that "A Daily School is a great desideratum". Desirable it may have been but there was still no day school providing an adequate education twenty-five years later. However, at the end of 1870, following the Education Act, the Elstow Vestry Meeting decided that the ratepayers should guarantee the sum of £200 towards a school, "Mr S C Whitbread having kindly agreed to find £250 and the site for a building". With this money guaranteed they could apply for a government grant towards the cost of building a school and a rate of one shilling in the pound was "agreed upon as a fair means of raising the sum required". Bureaucratic wheels must have ground just as slowly then as now because it was another three years before a school board was actually set up and the building was finally erected.

The small school at Wilstead had, by 1844, become "a poor room kept by an inefficient master" but there was "hope of a new room being built". With the aid of a grant from the National Society this hope soon became a reality and in 1852 an inspector could report that there was an "excellent building" and that the school was run by an "intelligent and painstaking" schoolmaster. A separate infant school was provided in 1873 by the Rev Lord John Thynne.

The provision of schools in England had developed in a piecemeal fashion over the century and in 1902 the government decided to abolish school boards and instead local education authorities were set up under the newly formed County Councils. Voluntary (or church) schools had the option of remaining as they were or giving up their church connections and becoming local authority schools. Finding the cost of the improvements required by new government standards to be beyond their means many gave up their voluntary status and among them were Southill, Cardington, Broom and Stanford. In 1903 the Bedfordshire Education Committee was formed and it was fitting, in view of his family's interest in and concern with education for more than a century, and their contribution to the provision of schools in the neighbourhood, that at its inaugural meeting Alderman Samuel Howard Whitbread was elected as its first chairman.

Church life in the nineteenth century

When churches are constantly trying to raise money for building repairs, when vicars look after groups of parishes and chapels close for lack of support, we are sometimes tempted to look at the past through rose-coloured spectacles and think of the last century as a time of sound buildings, with a vicar in every parish, and flourishing nonconformist chapels. But in fact it was not always quite like that.

Not all parishes have always had a vicar to themselves and on the Whitbread Estate Southill itself was a united benefice with Old Warden for 70 years, from 1797 until 1867. The vicar actually lived in Old Warden, the smaller of the two villages, and for the latter part of this time there was also a curate, who did not live in either village. Another incumbent, the Rev John Wing, held both Elstow and Stevington for 17 years, from 1832 to 1849.

The parish churches of all three villages needed major restoration work during or just after the nineteenth century – pictures of Elstow church in the eighteenth century show it in a very dilapidated state – but the congregations of those times were very fortunate in that the Whitbread family paid for the complete restoration of Elstow and of Cardington (which finally turned out to be not so much a restoration, more of a rebuilding) and for the repair of the chancel at Southill. The cost of restoring the nave of Southill (the responsibility of the parish) was raised by selling annuities, though this proved eventually to be a very expensive way of raising the capital, as even the shortest-lived annuitant did not die until she was 65, and all the rest lived to a far greater age.

Apart from these restorations other, less extensive repairs still needed to be done from time to time and for these, until a change in the law in 1868, the churchwardens could levy a church rate which was payable by all householders – Anglican, nonconformist and Catholic alike. In Elstow, for instance, this seemed to be either $1^1/_2$d or 2d in the pound for many years. Southill charged 3d in the pound in 1857 but this had gone down to 2d by 1868. Wealthy residents sometimes gave donations and another source of income was pew rents. In 1851 Cardington had 150 rented seats and Elstow 30, but there does not appear to be any record of the number at Southill at the time.

With the loss of revenue which followed the abolition of church rates in 1868 another source of income for church expenses had to be found, and the idea of regular offertory collections was introduced. The Bishop of Ely, in whose diocese Bedfordshire then was, was asked if he was in agreement with this and replied that he was. Elstow Vestry Meeting thereupon considered the proposal in 1881 and decided that a collection should be taken at least twice a year! A regular item on the agenda at the Annual Vestry Meeting there was the voting of money for the Singers' Feast, presumably their equivalent of a choir outing. For many years this was to cost no more than £1, but gradually the amount crept up, rising by ten shillings every few years.

The Whitbread family had their own pews at both Cardington and Southill. The one in the old St Mary's church at Cardington had a fireplace in it and one member of the family, born in 1863, remembered seeing her Uncle Charles poking the fire and putting coal on when she was a child. There was a family pew, too, at the west end of All Saints' at Southill. When the staff of the estate went to church a rigid hierarchy was observed in the seating arrangements, from the Agent's pew down to the seats of the humblest maids. The Sunday School children sat in the chancel, under the vigilant eye of the vicar's wife, and the choir was up in the organ loft. One old lady, recalling services from her childhood in the 1890s, remembered that the church was lit by smelly oil lamps and the aroma when the onion peelers from the hamlets of Stanford and Broom came to church was nauseating.

In spite of the establishment of a number of nonconformist chapels many of their members had to travel considerable distances to attend a chapel of their own persuasion or one where they saw eye-to-eye with the minister. As one minister put it, their congregations came from all the "circumjacent villages". They also had to support their ministers financially and many of the regular worshippers paid a rent for their pews. When the Wesleyan chapel was opened at Cardington in 1823 nearly all the 40 seats available for renting were let and by 1854 the annual rent for a pew was £5.

Over the years the numbers in a congregation fluctuated and there were times when chapels feared they would have to close because of lack of support. Cardington Wesleyans in the 1830s and Southill Baptists in the 1840s were both in this situation, but both survived, the Wesleyans until 1973 and the Baptists until the present day. For those who remained faithful to these causes the whole of Sunday was taken up with attending chapel, for there were services both in the morning and afternoon. If they had to travel some distance they took their lunch with them, sometimes in a basket kept specially for this purpose, and ate it in their pew or in the vestry. For one family it was usually "a raised pork pie, or sandwiches, or sausage rolls, with cake or pastry or bread and cheese. A bottle of beer was sent over for each family from the village inn where our horses were put up". Not all horses were put up at the local inn, for some chapels had their own stabling. It was not only the congregation who had to travel, but ministers and preachers often covered a good many miles on a Sunday.

Elstow Bunyan Meeting Sunday School Treat, c.1906

Before the days of compulsory school attendance the only education many children received was in the Sunday Schools. Even where a weekday school existed, as at Cardington and Southill, many children had to work on weekdays, and their only chance of learning to read would be at a Sunday School. They would spend most of the day there and at Cardington, for example, were expected to arrive punctually at nine o'clock in the morning, clean and "decently apparelled". In the summer they had a long break in the middle of the day and returned to the school until the early evening, but in winter they had a shorter break and went home in the early afternoon, before it got dark. For many of the children this was where they acquired their basic skills of reading and, sometimes, writing, although the education naturally had a religious bias. When Board schools were established in the 1870s and the children had to attend these every day the nature of the Sunday Schools changed and they concentrated on religious instruction. Sunday School treats became one of the highlights of the year and head teachers not infrequently commented in the school log books that attendances were poor on the day of a Sunday School treat. Sunday School anniversaries were another important annual event in the nonconformist church calendars, and a Cardington man remembered that the great event of the year at his chapel was the Annual Missionary Meeting, especially if a missionary was able to come and address them.

Inevitably there were the odd disagreements and personality clashes. The Street family of Harrowden fell out with the minister of Cotton End Meeting in the 1850s and transferred their allegiance to St Mary's Wesleyan Chapel in Bedford. There was a long drawn out dispute between the ratepayers and the vicar at Southill in the 1850s over the question of where certain parish records should be kept. At Elstow, when the Rev John Wing introduced a new parish clerk from Stevington into the parish church and the old one refused to go, the congregation took sides and there was a riot at the church.

Though church attendance was not quite as universal in Victorian days as we are sometimes inclined to think, still the churches and chapels were an important focus of spiritual and social life in the villages, and the Anglican services, at least, often reflected the events of national life. Reading through copies of forms of service for special occasions preserved from Cardington Church is like reading an outline history of the 19th century. Beginning with the Thanksgiving for the Defeat of the French in 1798 they include, among other events, the Escape of the King from Attack in 1800, the King's Recovery from Illness in 1801, the Safe Delivery of the Queen and the Birth of a Princess in 1840, The Prevalence of Cholera in this Country in 1849 and, finally, the Golden and Diamond Jubilees of Queen Victoria.

School life in the nineteenth century

From 1863 onwards, in schools which received a government grant, the head teacher was required by law to keep a log book, and many of these books still survive. In them were recorded the names of children admitted, lessons and subjects taught, accidents and epidemics (and sometimes deaths), problems with buildings, the appointment of teachers and inspectors' reports. As grants to schools were made on a "payment by results" basis (the idea is not new) inspectors' reports on the pupils' standards were of crucial importance.

From the log books it is clear that before school attendance was made compulsory, getting some of the children into school at all was not easy. There were parents who kept their children away because they needed the pittance their children could earn to help support the whole family; there were others who did not see the need for education; and there was always some children's natural inclination to truancy anyway. Reasons for absence that occurred regularly in Elstow, Cardington and Southill were haymaking, gleaning, potato picking, onion pulling, or whatever was the local employment of the season. Attendances when school re-opened in September were always poor everywhere – inevitably a lot of children were still helping with the harvest. Girls, of course, were often kept at home to work at lace-making or straw-plaiting at any time of the year.

At a time when many children had a long walk to get to school and their clothing was often inadequate, heavy rain, or ice and snow in winter, always kept a number of them away. Then there were the epidemics that broke out periodically, when poor attendances and the risk of infection sometimes forced schools to close and sometimes there were deaths among the pupils. At Elstow in 1887 there was scarlet fever (scarlatina) in the village and three children in the infants' class died in the early months of the following year. Two years before that the headmaster's daughter had died, probably of whooping cough. The log book contains only the simple statement that "The Master's child was buried on Wednesday afternoon, consequently there was no school".

In Southill and its hamlet of Stanford in 1892 there was even an outbreak of typhoid as well as scarlet fever. Two children in Southill also died of diphtheria in the winter of 1892-3 and another time several children were away with the "Blister Pock" (?chicken-pox). When an outbreak of diphtheria occurred at Broom Infants' School and some of the older children, who attended Southill

Children on Elstow Green

School, were told to stay at home, the headmaster at Southill seemed as much concerned over the effect the absences would have on the inspectors' reports, and hence on his grants, as about the danger of spreading the infection.

Not all pupils' absences were for such serious reasons. Fairs, Sunday School treats and such entertainments were a great temptation and headmasters seemed resigned to the inevitability of the situation when they wrote that attendances were poor because of a fair or regatta in Bedford, affecting Elstow, or a fair in a neighbouring village, which affected Southill. A rather more unusual reason for absences was a "pigeon match over the school", which the Elstow headmaster once blamed for poor attendance. With the appointment of school attendance officers in the 1880s the amount of absence from school declined, and it was one problem less for the headmaster to deal with.

Legitimate holidays were shorter than they are now and were set by the local governors. Elstow children seem to have had more "casual" days off than those at Southill, having regular holidays for the Elstow fairs in May and November and for various other days. There was always either a half-holiday or school would finish early for the "annual maypole" on the village green. At Southill, the school being a church school, the pupils went regularly to church on Ash Wednesday and Ascension Day, sometimes having a half-holiday afterwards.

Because the amount of the grants schools received depended largely on examination results instruction tended to concentrate on teaching the 3Rs, but geography, history, science and religious knowledge were also taught in all the local schools and all the girls had needlework lessons. Singing was sometimes mentioned and at Southill the children "showed a great liking for musical drill". Inspectors' reports showed the educational standards reached were not very high, though they were probably similar to those in the rest of the county.

One inspector who came here from Yorkshire found the children "inferior in physique to the northern children" (no doubt because of the widespread poverty in rural Bedfordshire at that time) and some inspectors believed that their lack of physical stamina was the cause of their "mental inertia" and "having no appetite for knowledge". Nevertheless it was concluded that Bedfordshire children could hold their own "when properly taught".

Pupils' misdemeanours, and the consequent punishments, were recorded too and it is noticeable that all the reports in the Elstow and Southill log books (Cardington's is not available) concern boys. Perhaps the girls were better-behaved! Caning was the punishment most often meted out, though there were occasional expulsions. One boy was expelled from Southill for "gross misconduct", but we can only speculate as to what this might have been – the headmaster gave no further details, nor did he record the reason for caning two boys "on the seat" some time later. The Elstow headmaster was obviously trying to make the punishment fit the crime when he caught a boy lying about the reason for his lateness, and "set him to learn a text on the dangers of lying". But the boy found walking on the wall was caned and others who climbed the school walls when they had just been repaired also received punishment, though what form it took was not specified.

When attendance was compulsory and until government funding made schooling free the collection of school fees caused head teachers a few headaches from time to time. Now and again a parent would refuse to pay the school pence and a heated argument would follow. At Elstow the School Board ruled that all fees must be paid on Monday morning and in 1889 they set the fees at two pence a week for the first child in the family and one penny per child afterwards, up to a maximum of sixpence a week for any one family, but not all schools adopted this "cheaper by the dozen" approach. Farmers were required to pay three pence a week for each child (at one time it had been as much as sixpence) and it was common for farmers to be expected to pay more. At Southill the vicar came to the school to collect the school pence.

The condition of the buildings was another recurring problem. All the schools seem to have had trouble with their stoves and keeping the classrooms warm in the winter was often difficult – it sometimes seemed to be a choice between shivering with cold or choking from the smoke. On one memorable occasion at Southill the classroom temperature was 28 degrees Fahrenheit and the ink was frozen. Small wonder that 17 children were absent. The school had to be closed for two weeks while one new stove was installed and the others repaired, and Cardington and Elstow had similar difficulties. The earth closets also caused problems. There is a long entry in the Elstow School log book about the ones there, for which ashes were used. They were obviously a constant source of unpleasantness and worry, and the poor headmaster complained that "bad smells are common".

Even though Elstow School was a board school the local vicar was a frequent visitor and at Southill, as well as the vicar, Lady Isabella Whitbread paid regular visits which were all carefully noted in the log book. On one occasion she spoke to the children about their poor attendance record and the bad examination results that had followed. But perhaps they did not heed her warnings sufficiently, because only a few years afterwards an inspector threatened that "Unless much improvement is effected in the Current School Year, Her Majesty's Inspector may be compelled to report the School inefficient under Article 86". Fortunately that never seems to have happened.

The Twentieth Century

Church life changed very little in the first years of this century, but gradually Sunday worship became a more comfortable affair. Smoky stoves were replaced by central heating, electric light was put into most churches and chapels some time round about 1930, and the organist no longer needed someone to pump the bellows when an electric organ blower had been installed. Coal bills and payments to the lad who pumped the bellows disappeared from the account books. In some churches old seating was removed and replaced with more comfortable pews or chairs.

Paying for these improvements, as well as coping with the normal upkeep of the buildings, meant that money was always needed. In Anglican churches the collections, which had been quarterly or even less frequent when first introduced, were stepped up to being first monthly and then weekly. Most churches received gifts of furniture or other items from time to time, but fund-raising bazaars and fêtes, which had begun to be a regular feature of church life in Victorian times, remained a favourite way of raising money. More recently the fund-raisers have had all sort of imaginative ideas. Elstow and Southill churches had *son et lumière* evenings and Elstow held a Vanity Fayre on the Green in 1988, the 300th anniversary of the death of John Bunyan. There have, of course, been numerous flower festivals and craft fairs everywhere. All Saints also had an "It's a Knock-out" competition between Southill, Stanford and Broom and an ingenious treasure hunt, "Goldfinger 82", in which the clues finally led the successful hunters to the inscription on Dilley's memorial in the church.

The service registers in the parish churches show how the pattern of their Sunday services has changed over the century. Communion services, not always held every Sunday, were always said, not sung, in the early days, usually at 8.00 am, and sometimes also after matins or evensong. Matins at 11 o'clock was the main service of the day and there was a regular evensong at six or six-thirty. At Cardington the choirboys went to Sunday School in the building now occupied by the Bedfordshire Road Cycling Club at 9.30 am, and then ran across the green to put on their surplices to sing at matins at eleven. Sung eucharist began to be introduced in the post-war years, and has largely become the main service on Sundays, often at 9.30 am, and evensong is now far less common.

Until well after the last war most children went to Sunday School, partly for the social activities as well as for religious instruction (and in many cases to give their parents an hour or two of peace and quiet) and the numbers attending seem to have reached a peak in the fifties almost everywhere, but since then attendances have fallen drastically. Among the youth groups there were the Cardington

Wesleyans' Band of Hope, which was thriving before 1914, but "fell away" during World War I, and a group called the Brisstles, started in the 1980s for the youngsters of Broom, Southill and Stanford.

About the turn of the century the three parish churches all needed to extend their churchyards. Southill obviously had difficulty in looking after such a large area, and when the vicar complained to the P C C in 1920 about the state of the churchyard they suggested looking into the possibility of putting sheep in there to keep the grass down, at which Mr Whitbread said he would arrange for this to be done if the idea proved practicable. Southill P C C, it should be noted, was by this time meeting in the sober surroundings of either the Vicarage or Southill House, unlike some of their predecessors who, for many years prior to 1895, met in the White Horse !

The extension to the burial ground at Cardington was across the road from the church and the original churchyard, and it was here that the men who died in the R101 airship disaster in 1930 were buried. After a state procession from Westminster, the bodies were brought by train to St John's station in Bedford and taken in procession to Cardington, where the funeral service ended as dusk fell on what must have been a very long and tiring day for the mourners. For fifty years an annual memorial service was held in Cardington Church on the anniversary of the disaster, the last one being held in October 1981.

The outbreak of war in 1939 brought the problem of blacking out large church windows and it was common to find the time of evensong altered from six o'clock to three o'clock, though from 1938 Southill Baptist Church had, in any case, been "mainly an afternoon ministry" because of the difficulty of getting ministers. Outside the churches iron gates and railings were removed for recycling for munitions and armaments.

The 1950s saw two Wesleyan congregations establish new chapels at Stanford and at Broom, where they converted a redundant school into an "exceedingly comfortable House of Worship", as *The Biggleswade Chronicle* called it. But the period of expansion was soon over, and between the mid-sixties and the mid-eighties Harrowden, Cardington, Broom and Stanford Methodist chapels all closed. Cardington Wesleyans joined with the Howard Union Church, just across the road, which had by then become a United Reformed Church. It had left its converted barn and moved into a handsome new building in Cople Road in 1908. For the last ten years or so the number of places of worship has remained stable and there have been no more closures of churches or chapels of any denomination.

As with church life, school life really altered very little in the first years of the century. Schools were still cold – Cardington recorded frozen ink and a classroom temperature of 32 degrees in January 1912, and problems with the stoves continued. One advantage of the stoves, though, in the days before school dinners, was that they were ideal for baking potatoes. Children who had a long way to go to school would take a large potato for baking and at Cardington, at any rate, they could keep a tin of cocoa at school, marked with their name, so that with their baked potato and cocoa they were provided with something hot to eat and drink in the middle of the day.

Cardington School had in fact been given a dire report in 1904 which condemned the premises as dirty and unsatisfactory and the staff as inefficient. After that standards gradually went up, but unfortunately the numbers went down and by the 1920s it took children up to the age of eleven only, the older ones going to Elstow. There was a short period, though, at the beginning of the Second World War, when it went back to being an all-age school.

The little schools at Broom and Stanford (the latter was only in existence from 1899 to 1921) were built for young children up to the age of seven to save them walking to Southill every day, and some of the children were actually as young as three. Stanford School had just one teacher; Broom, having more children, had a headmistress and an assistant. Both places seem to have been friendly, caring little schools and the inspectors referred to Stanford as "a really excellent little school" and to Broom as being "conducted with a kindly understanding of small children". One former pupil recalls the last teacher at Stanford giving the children "dolly mixtures" on Friday afternoons, and always letting them sleep on until they woke naturally from their afternoon nap, however late it was. But it seems unlikely that there were many recruits for the church choir from Stanford, judging from the teacher's rather despairing comment that the children had "such poor voices for singing".

The First World War appears to have had little impact on school life, the only real difference it seemed to make was that schools were closed for an extra week now and then so that the pupils could help with work on the farms.

The headmasters of the day were, according to reports, strict. One of the masters at Southill, Mr J B Jones (strict but fair) was a keen gardener and under him the boys were taught gardening, planning the crops in winter and working outside in their own gardens, near the church, in the better weather. Mr Jones was also keen on cricket and reading, and would read to the boys while the girls concentrated on their sewing lessons.

It was in the 1920s that the Elstow headmaster, Mr Wadsworth (very strict) revived the May Day celebrations on the village green and these were looked forward to eagerly by the girls, who thought practising for the maypole dancing was far more enjoyable than normal lessons. Added to which there was the excitement of new dresses for the occasion. The girls who attended the Bunyan Meeting Sunday School would put theirs away carefully after the dancing in readiness for the Sunday School anniversary later in the year.

In between the wars the doctor and the dentist became regular visitors to the school. There were annual medical inspections and also dental inspections, which were usually more frequent. The dentist would come one day to examine the children's teeth and return later to carry out any necessary treatment at the school – and there was no anaesthetic for fillings in those days, either. It was during this period, too, that there were references to children going to Bedford to sit for examinations for places at the grammar schools there.

The Second World War had a much greater effect on school life than the First, particularly at Southill and Broom, where there were a lot of evacuees. Broom School, where numbers in 1939 were only half what they had been in 1900, was full again and there were extra teachers. The Assembly Room at Broom was also brought into use as a classroom to cope with the extra numbers from Southill School, which was bursting at the seams. Space there was at such a premium that a shift system of schooling had to be introduced, half the pupils having lessons in the morning and the other half in the afternoon. Elstow, too, had evacuees from the National Children's Home in London, though not nearly so many as Southill. All the schools had to practise air-raid drill at the outbreak of war and in April 1940 Cardington could claim that every child was under cover in 5-6 minutes. Air raid warnings in the area were not infrequent in late 1940 and early 1941.

With the end of the war the evacuees went home and at Broom School there were few pupils left. When the inevitable end came and the school closed in 1948 there were just five children remaining. The building became Broom Methodist Chapel and was used for another quarter of a century before it was eventually demolished and a house built on the site.

Changes in the education system since the war have meant that only children up to the age of nine go to school in the villages (the older ones go to Bedford or Shefford) and since 1982 there has been no school at all in Cardington. Today the schools are warm, bright, cheerful places, equipped with all the up-to-date technology – television, video recorders and computers. Children are not expected to walk long distances to school any more, the cane has been put away and the dentist doesn't use a room in the school as a surgery these days. Inspectors, however, still come regularly and there is a newcomer too, the school photographer, whose annual visits are, no doubt, recorded in the log books. For

Broom Methodist Chapel, once Broom School, now demolished

log books, like inspectors, are still a part of the school scene.

Two hundred years after Samuel Whitbread I bought Southill House there are still parish churches in Southill, Cardington and Elstow, and three nonconformist churches which are the descendants of the Independent Meeting Houses in Southill and Cardington Cotton End, and the group in Cardington for whom John Howard had a cottage "adapted for religious purposes". Just one Methodist church has survived, at Wilstead, and there is also the Bunyan Meeting at Elstow. There are three village schools, in Southill, Elstow and Cotton End, instead of the scattering of small schools in the area two hundred years ago, and Wilstead still has its own school. Put like that the situation doesn't sound all that different from what it was in 1795. Southill is even sharing a vicar again, although now with the parish of Clifton. But in reality, of course, things are very different. The buildings themselves have all changed. Some have been restored and some rebuilt, and there are others which are entirely new. More importantly, the life that has gone on within those buildings has changed, and is still changing, particularly in the schools. Samuel Whitbread II's vision of education for all children has become a reality, and the village schools his descendants helped to establish are part of a whole world of educational opportunity far beyond anything he could ever have imagined.

CHURCH AND SCHOOL LIFE

NONCONFORMIST CHURCHES WITHIN THE SOUTHILL ESTATE

BAPTIST

Cardington Cotton End. 1776. New chapel built 1836. Still in use.
Southill. c.1700. New Meeting House built 1805. Still in use.
Note: Both of these chapels began as Independent Meetings, and became Baptist Congregations in the nineteenth century.

METHODIST

Southill, Broom. 1950. Congregation had held weekly evening service in the Broom Assembly Room (village hall) since the beginning of this century, or possibly the 1890s. A member bought Broom Infants' School when it became redundant in 1948 and rented it to the church. Dedicated February 1950. Closed 1976. Demolished.
Southill, Stanford. 1956. Chapel in rented premises. Closed c. 1986.
Cardington. 1823. Closed 1973. Now a private house. Congregation joined the members of the Howard Union Church (URC) in Cardington in 1985.
Cardington, Harrowden. 1904. Closed mid-1960s. Now private house.
Wilstead. 1808. New buildings 1847 and 1967. Still in use.

CONGREGATIONAL

Cardington: Howard Union Church. First met before 1796 in a cottage John Howard had had adapted "for religious purposes". Moved to a converted barn rented from Mr Whitbread in 1839 and given this name. New church built in 1908. As a Congregational Church became part of the United Reformed Church. Joined by Cardington Wesleyans when their church closed. Sharing agreement signed 1985.

BUNYAN MEETING

Elstow. From 1811 onwards met in the upper floor of the Green House (the Moot Hall). New church built 1910. Still in use.

Chapter 7

Whitbread Monuments and Memorials

by LINDA SWAIN

THIS VOLUME IS intended to celebrate the two hundred years the Whitbread family have owned the Southill estate, and in this section we can discover how their local involvement is shown in gifts to and monuments in the churches linked to that estate. Of these, the church of St Mary Cardington is the richest source. History shows that the Whitbread family progressed from being prosperous yeomen in the middle ages to county gentry in the nineteenth century, using the wealth from the London brewery founded by Samuel Whitbread I, and the family kept its local influence and popularity by its support for good housing, for schools, and for local churches and nonconformist congregations.

The family bought land in Cardington in the reign of Charles I and moved to live there from their old home at Ion in Upper Gravenhurst in 1650, or so we are told on a large marble tablet below a monument erected by Ive Whitbread in 1750 on the west wall of the Whitbread chapel in the north transept of Cardington church. The date of his own death was added to the memorial in 1766. The inscription claims descent from a Norman companion of William the Conqueror, for which statement there is no other evidence. In addition to various births, marriages and deaths, the text records also the service of William Whitbread to the Parliamentary cause in the Civil War, as well as his later service as Receiver General and Justice of the Peace, before his death on 4 August 1701 at the age of 74 years. He outlived his wife Lettice, who had died 4 June 1698, aged 69.

On the east wall of the chapel is an equally large monument by H Weekes, of 1849, to Samuel Whitbread II, the politician and Member of Parliament for Bedford, who died 6 July 1815, and also to his wife Elizabeth, who died 28 November 1846.

On the north wall of the chapel is an impressive monument of 1799 by John

Memorial in Cardington Church to Samuel Whitbread I, by John Bacon, 1799

Bacon, R A, to Samuel Whitbread I who died in June 1796, and below is a brass plaque in memory of William Whitbread, who died on 12 June 1879, just before his 45th birthday. He was the second son of Samuel Charles and Juliana Whitbread, and the plaque was erected by his wife and five children.

To the right of these memorials is a simple, dignified tablet erected "by her husband and five surviving children" to the memory of Juliana Whitbread, who died 13 October 1858, just before her 54th birthday, after "protracted suffering".

To balance this, to the left of the monument to Samuel I, is another tablet which records the tragic accidental death of Charles Samuel and Juliana's infant

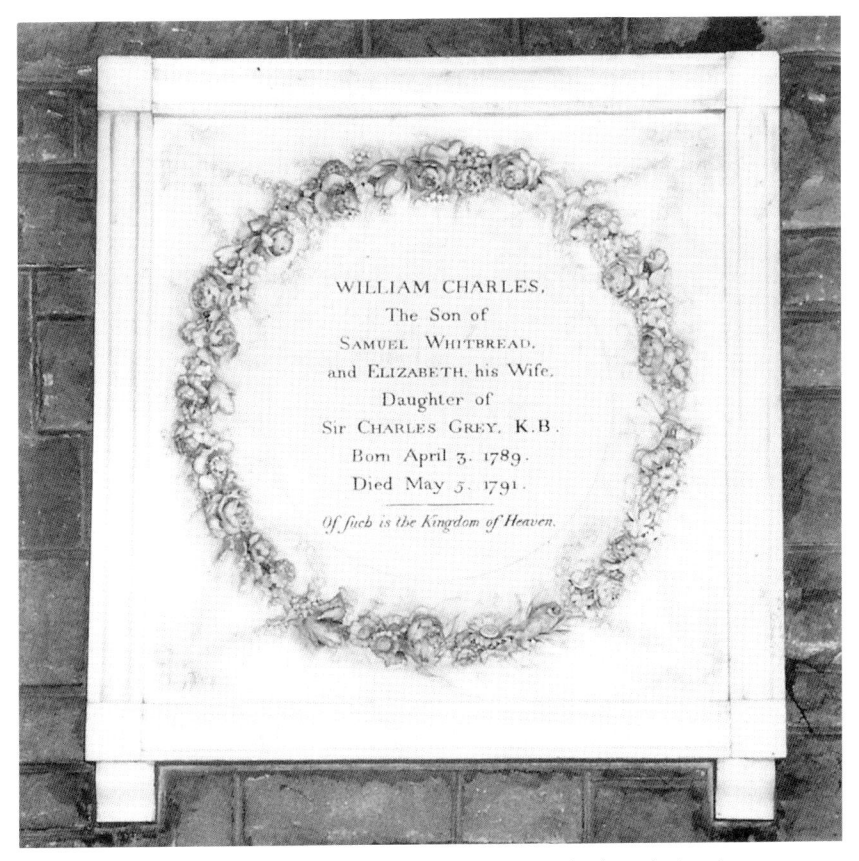

> WILLIAM CHARLES,
> The Son of
> SAMUEL WHITBREAD,
> and ELIZABETH, his Wife,
> Daughter of
> Sir CHARLES GREY, K.B.
> Born April 3. 1789.
> Died May 5. 1791.
>
> *Of such is the Kingdom of Heaven.*

Memorial in Cardington Church to William Charles Whitbread

son Charles, killed on 31 July 1845 by a falling tree on the Cardington estate.

In the south chapel, on the floor, can be seen a ledger stone marking the burial place of Henry Whitbread, who died 13 October 1727 aged 62; his first wife Sarah, who died 27 December 1710, aged 36; and his second wife, Elizabeth, who outlived him, dying on 9 January 1746/7, aged 59.

A smaller paving slab marks the last resting-place of Henry and Sarah's second son John, who died a bachelor on 12 February 1762, at the age of 67; his elder brother William, who died 16 July 1721 aged 28; his younger sister Lettice died on 21 December 1721 aged 25; and a still younger sister, Sarah, died 10 March 1699/1700 aged only 11 months.

In the north east angle of the wall is a handsome monument, a bust of General

Charles James Conway Mills, who died on 12 February 1894 aged 77 years. He was a soldier of distinction decorated for the part he played at the siege of Sebastopol in the Crimean War. His wife, Gertrude, the second daughter of Samuel Charles and Juliana Whitbread, lived until 1909.

On the east wall of the chapel, to the right of the window, another marble wall-plaque, with a wreath of roses and other flowers carved in high relief, tells of the loss to Samuel Whitbread II and his wife Lady Elizabeth of their first child, William Charles, who died on 5 May 1791, one month after his second birthday. In this instance, no cause of death is recorded, but it was a time where there was all too little defence against the usual childhood diseases.

In the chancel the striking east window, perpendicular in style, has ten principal lights arranged in two rows of five. The upper five depict the Crucifixion, and the lower five tell the story of the Good Samaritan. It was designed and made by the well-known Victorian firm of Clayton and Bell. As recorded on the adjacent wall-plaque, it is in memory of William Henry Whitbread, who died in 1867, having served as M P for Bedford from 1818-1834, and later as Sheriff for the county. The window was given by his widow, Harriet.

On the south wall of the chancel is a dignified white tablet, surmounted by an urn, at the base of which are three children, carved in relief. These no doubt represent the three children mentioned in the text, which tells us that Harriot, the first wife of Samuel Whitbread I, died on Easter Day 22 April 1764, aged only 29, leaving two young daughters and a baby son. Adjacent to it, to the right of the east window, is an elegant white urn, carved in relief, surmounted by a putto, the whole enclosed in a narrow oval border of dark marble. The inscription tells us that it is a memorial to Lady Mary Whitbread, second wife of Samuel Whitbread I. She died 27 December 1770 aged 34, after giving birth to a daughter, Mary, who survived her, a consolation to the doubly bereaved Samuel.

Of Harriot's two daughters, the younger, Emma Maria Elizabeth, is commemorated by another wall-plaque, on the north wall of the chancel, recording her death at the age of 62 on 10 July 1825, by which time she was the widow of Henry Beauchamp, Lord St John of Bletsoe.

On the chancel floor can be seen the ledger stone which marks the burial place of Samuel Whitbread I, who died 11 June 1796 aged 75.

Although not memorials, there are many other items, gifts to the church by the Whitbread family over many years. There is, over the door, the carpet-work coat-of-arms of King George III, dated 1799, made and presented by Mary Whitbread, daughter of Samuel Whitbread I, who also made and presented a similar coat-of-arms, dated 1778, at Essendon, in Hertfordshire, where Samuel

Memorial to Samuel Whitbread II and the Wedgwood Font, Cardington Church by Bernard West

Whitbread I had his country seat at Bedwell Park.

The black basalt font, not now standing on its original black basalt base but on a square, tapering, fluted pillar, is today in the Whitbread chapel in the north transept, where so many of the family are buried. It was made in the Wedgwood factory at Etruria, near Stoke-on-Trent. This was the gift of Harriot Whitbread in 1783, and similar ones were given by her sisters to the parish churches of Essendon in Hertfordshire, and of Melchbourne, Bedfordshire, the latter at the time of Emma's marriage to Lord St John of Bletsoe. The Melchbourne font is now in America. One other such font is known to exist. It was once at St

Margaret's Moreton, Salop., but is now in the Lady Lever Art Gallery at Port Sunlight.

The former clock on the tower was the joint gift of Samuel Whitbread I and his cousin John Howard in 1760. Also gifts of Samuel Whitbread are the communion plate given in 1763, and the Parish Library, established by him in 1787-8, housed in the old vicarage built by him in 1781. When the original five bells were re-cast in 1772, by the firm of Pack and Chapman of Whitechapel, he gave an additional one, and two more were added by Samuel Whitbread II in 1785 to commemorate his coming of age in that year. This gave Cardington the fourth ring of eight bells in Bedfordshire, and it is considered to be one of the finest village peals in the county. They were again recast during the 1897-1901 re-building, this time by the well-known bell-founders John Taylor and Company of Loughborough, making them among the earliest rings in the country to be cast, tuned and hung on modern principles.

There are two lecterns in the church. The earlier, in brass, was given by Lady Isabella Whitbread at the time of the rebuilding at the end of the nineteenth century, and now stands at the back of the church. The one in current use is of wood, designed by the late Sir Albert Richardson, and the eagle carved by Frank Dobson, R A. It was given in 1955 by Mr Humphrey Whitbread.

The pulpit dates from 1901, and was a joint gift from Mrs C Mills and Miss Elizabeth Whitbread, sisters of Samuel Whitbread III. A major gift was the work carried out between 1897 and 1905, initially intended to be a restoration, but in the end a rebuilding of the whole church except for the chancel. The whole cost was met by Samuel Whitbread III, who also provided workmen from the Southill estate to carry out the work under the supervision of George Highton, the Diocesan Surveyor.

Moving on to the church of All Saints, Southill, we find another fine east window, given in memory of William Henry Whitbread, who died in 1867, by his widow Harriet. Again, it is perpendicular in style, but this one has three principal lights and six tracery lights above, the latter filled with figures of saints. Below these, the central figure is of Jesus the Good Shepherd, flanked by the Sower and the Reaper.

On the south side of the chancel is a single lancet window, filled with stained glass, dedicated to the memory of W H Whitbread's widow, Harriet, who died 6 February 1871. The subject is inspired by Job 29, and shows a woman, carrying a child in her arms, dispensing bread to children.

At the west end of the south aisle, another perpendicular window has twentieth century stained glass given in memory of (Anne) Joscelyne Whitbread, who died in 1936, aged 29. She was the daughter of Samuel Howard Whitbread, Lord Lieutenant of Bedfordshire and the first wife of her cousin William Henry Whitbread, who re-married during the second World War. The design of the window is simple, but very effective. Apart from the inscription, the only decoration is of a dove, the usual symbol of the Holy Spirit, descending and radiating light. It is neither dated nor signed, but a faculty of 1937 gives the designer as Hugh Easton.

Nearby is a font of simple modern design by Sir Albert Richardson. This was installed in 1937, and around the rim is inscribed the name of Joscelyne Whitbread.

Across the west end of the church is a splendid wooden gallery, supporting the organ above it, and incorporating the Whitbread family pew below. An inscription on the central panel of the gallery states that in 1814-16 extensive alterations and repairs were undertaken at the expense of the parishioners, and under the auspices of Samuel Whitbread Esq. and the Vicar and Churchwardens. The organ was the gift of the first William Henry Whitbread in 1867, installed by the firm of Walker of Tottenham Court Road, London.

The third church association with the Whitbread estate is the Abbey Church of St Mary and St Helena. It contains no Whitbread memorials, though the family has born the cost of restoration and repairs.

Ive Whitbread's monument in Cardington Church

IVE WHITBREAD ESQR. OF THIS PARISH AND OF THE CITY OF LONDON MERCHANT ERECTED THIS MONUMENT / TO THE MEMORY OF HIS ANCESTORS WHO COMING INTO ENGLAND WITH THE NORMANS / SETTLED AT ION HOUSE IN THE PARISH OF UPPER GRAVENHURST IN THIS COUNTY OF BEDFORD / UPON AN ESTATE GIVEN THEM BY THE CONQUEROR AND CONTINUED THERE UNTIL THE YEAR 1650 / WHEN WILLIAM WHITBREAD ESQR. / PURCHASED LANDS AND SETTLED IN THIS TOWN OF CARDINGTON WHERE THE FAMILY HAVE EVER / SINCE CONTINUED AND MANY OF THEM UPON THEIR DECEASE HAVE BEEN INTERRED IN THIS CHURCH / HIS ELDEST SON HENRY WHITBREAD ESQR. SUCCEEDED AND AFTER HIM / HIS ELDEST SON WILLIAM WHITBREAD ESQR. / WHO ESPOUSED THE CAUSE OF HIS COUNTRY IN THE REIGN OF KING CHARLES THE FIRST / AND ACCEPTING OF A COMMISSION IN THE ARMY BEHAVED WITH THE GREATEST COURAGE AND GALLANTRY / AND WAS

MANY YEARS RECEIVER GENERAL AND JUSTICE OF THE PEACE FOR THIS COUNTY / HE MARRIED LETTICE DAUGHTER OF EDWARD LEEDS OF CROXTON IN THE COUNTY OF CAMBRIDGE ESQR. / BY WHOM HE HAD TWO SONS AND SIX DAUGHTERS / SHE DIED 4 JUNE 1698 AGED 69 YEARS. HE DIED 4 AUGT. 1701 AGED 74 YEARS / HIS ELDEST SON HENRY WHITBREAD ESQR. / SUCCEEDED TO HIS ESTATES AND OFFICE OF RECEIVER GENERAL AND FIRST MARRIED SARAH DAUGHTER AND / COHEIRESS OF JOHN IVE OF LONDON MERCHANT AND HAD BY HER THREE SONS AND THREE DAUGHTERS / SHE DIED 27 DECR. 1710 AGED 36 YEARS / HE DIED 13 OCTR. 1727 AGED 62 YEARS / SARAH 10 MARCH 1699 11 MONTHS WILLIAM DIED 16 JULY 1721 AGED 28 YEARS LETTICE 21 DECR. 1721 25 YEARS

     JOHN , IVE AND RACHEL ARE LIVING
HE MARRIED TO HIS SECOND WIFE ELIZABETH DAUGHTER OF PHILLIP READ OF NEW SARUM IN WILTS M.D. / AND HAD BY HER TWO SONS AND ONE DAUGHTER SHE DIED 9 JANY. 1746 AGED 59 YEARS / HENRY THE ELDEST SON DIED 22 APRIL 1742 AGED 22 YEARS / SAMUEL AND ELIZABETH ARE LIVING / MDCCL /

THE ABOVE MENTIONED JOHN WHITBREAD ESQR. DIED A BATCHELOR 12 FEBY. 1762 AGED 67 YEARS / RACHEL MARRIED OLIVER EDWARDS ESQR. OF THE CITY OF LONDON AND DIED 29 AUGT. 1757 AGED 66 YEARS / IVE WHITBREAD ESQR. ABOVE AND FIRST MENTIONED / MARRIED ELIZABETH DAUGHTER OF PETER HINDE OF THEOBALDS IN THE COUNTY OF HERTFORD ESQR. / HE DIED 7 MAY 1765 AGED 65 YEARS. SHE SURVIVED HIM ONLY TO 7 JULY 1766 AGED 46 YEARS / THEIR REMAINS ARE INTERRED UNDERNEATH / THEY HAD ONE DAUGHTER CATHARINE WHO DIED AN INFANT 13 JUNE 1748 / AND ONE SON JACOB NOW LIVING MDCCLXVI.

Chapter 8

The Midland Railway

by MARTIN LAWRENCE

THE COMING OF the railway to Bedfordshire heralded the dawn of the Victorian age in the county, the era of British industrial and imperial supremacy. Thackeray suggested that the railway embankment symbolized the great dividing line in the lives of his contemporaries. Those who could remember the prerailway age lived on, severed from the world of their youth. Many in Bedfordshire feared "the locomotive monster . . . navigated by a tail of smoke and sulphur". However, the county also contained one of the most ardent protagonists for the railway cause – William Henry Whitbread. Frustrated by a change in political tide, the former Whig MP for Bedford threw his considerable energies into the promotion of railways. He had a free trader's vision of the rapid movement of goods around the country and saw the commercial advantage that was to be gained. If his destiny was not to be in parliament, he would play his full part in the economic expansion of Britain through the growth in railway routes, particularly in linking the centres of midland industrial power to London. His plan placed the Southill estate at the heart of this development.

William Henry had been born on 4 February 1795, the eldest surviving son of Samuel Whitbread II and Lady Elizabeth (Grey). Educated at Eton and Trinity College Cambridge, he undertook a tour of the Continent appropriate for a young man of his wealth and position. At the tragic death of his father in 1815 he found himself the inheritor of substantial estates, a brewery fortune and political opportunity. That he never sought to capitalise on all of these gifts was not due to a lack of ability, but to a predispositon towards pursuing his own interests and projects. This independence of mind did not match the expectations of society at either national or local level, and in some senses he remained partially removed from the county social scene.

On his father's death he was aged only 20 and thus not able to succeed him as MP for Bedford, a parliamentary seat that appeared to be at the behest of the Whitbread family, for their candidature had not been contested for 25 years.

William Henry Whitbread by William Bradley, 1841

Captain Waldegrave, his brother-in-law, was elected without opposition and held the seat until the 1818 General Election, when he retired in favour of William Henry. There is no doubt about Whitbread's desire to serve as a Member of Parliament, and even after his defeat in 1835 he sought re-election in 1841. However, his motivation was to carry out his public duty for the Whig cause rather than for any personal political aspirations. As evidence, it is worth noting that he was scrupulous in avoiding the use of bribery to favour his candidature, a weapon that others used against him, and during his period in the House of Commons it is reported that he did not speak once in a debate. For Whitbread it was his vote that counted and the Great Reform Bill, the Emancipation of Slaves and Poor Law reform were all causes that he supported in the lobby.

The Whitbread family had moved into Southill House in 1800 and thus much of William's life had been spent there. He was interested in making a contribution to county life in more ways than representation in parliament. He thus engaged himself in the modernisation of agricultural methods on his estate, he supported schools, hospitals and church restoration, and played his full part as magistrate at petty and quarter sessions. As recreation, he hunted with the Oakley Hunt. He exemplified the Whig tradition, favouring free trade and a recognition of industrial and imperial concerns without embracing radical views which might alter the balance of rural society. He was diligent in his duties and philanthropic, if not particularly popular. He separated from his first wife and therefore had no hostess at Southill, and his staunch Whig views isolated him from his fellow squires, who were increasingly turning to the Tory party and protectionism.

The great passion of his life was his support for the cause of railways, into which he threw himself in a manner which dismayed some of Bedfordshire's foremost landowners. He had been a keen supporter of the *Bedford Times* Coach, which ran from Bedford *via* Hitchin to London. He recognised that railways would supplant the coaches and was anxious to be involved. Whitbread saw the Midland Railway Company as the means whereby he could influence railway development in the county and play an important role in its promotion.

The London to Birmingham line had opened in 1838, starting at Euston and running through Linslade and Bletchley on its way to the Midlands. It did not touch Bedfordshire, though the Linslade station was called Leighton Buzzard, and was much used by people in that part of the county. Bedford itself was 16 miles from the nearest station at Bletchley, and a branch line linking Bedford with Bletchley opened in 1846. On the other side of the county the Great Northern Line, opened in 1850, passed on its way northwards through Hitchin, Biggleswade and Sandy. However, Bedford itself was still not on a main line, and the inhabitants felt themselves gravely disadvantaged.

The Midland, under the leadership of George Hudson, 'the Railway King', had developed from four provincial companies whose lines all met at Derby. This amalgamation had taken place to facilitate the movement of passengers and goods to London. In 1845 the South Midland Railway had proposed a line from Leicester to Hitchin but the scheme had been rejected by the House of Commons.

In 1846 the Midland planned its line through Bedford to Hitchin. Hudson, the prime mover, chose Robert Stephenson as Chief Engineer with Charles Liddell as his assistant. The capital required was £2,250,000 and this was found difficult to raise because the Railway Mania of the period had exhausted the ready supply. The necessary Bill passed both Houses of Parliament, but the Midland Railway Company decided not to proceed. In 1850 their powers to extend the line expired. George Hudson had resigned the previous year over allegations of irregularities in the company accounts, and John Ellis became Chairman.

Whitbread had followed the situation carefully and, instead of being daunted, stepped up his campaign to route the railway through his estate. He owned one eighth of all the land needed for its construction. He wrote to John Ellis and offered the Midland Railway land at no more than £70 an acre, a modest price that the Midland found difficult to refuse. Furthermore, Whitbread was prepared to use the receipts from the sale of the land to further invest in the company. The sale was agreed and Whitbread increased his shareholding in the Midland Railway.

In 1852 an agreement was made between the Midland and the Great Northern to accommodate the former's traffic at Hitchin. The route was now re-surveyed by Charles Liddell and John Crossley. Liddell estimated that £304,000 would be needed to build the Hitchin to Bedford section alone. Once the Act received the Royal Assent on 4 August 1853, Thomas Brassey, the greatest of railway contractors, organised the construction which commenced in April 1854 on the estate in Cardington and Old Warden. Raising the capital remained difficult. The national economy was still struggling and with the onset of the Crimean War and investors were reluctant to take such risks. It is reported that John Ellis was forced to put a limit of £19,000 per mile on the cost of construction.

The company's difficulties were exacerbated further by the Crimean War when labour became short for construction work. Military service in war time became an acceptable alternative to navvying. The costs of material and of labour rose sharply and the Midland pressed for greater productivity from their men. Additional cost was caused by the language and conduct of the navvies. From July 1854 the company felt obliged to employ, at 200 guineas a year, several scripture readers to damp down the men's verbal enthusiasm. There was "irregular and riotous conduct" which resulted in the swearing in of special constables. Thieving and poaching was common among navvies, one of them being charged with stealing a sleeper received fourteen days hard labour as a first offence. Despite the fact that drunkenness was also common, it was necessary to have public houses near the construction works. Between Shefford and Cardington there was no conveniently placed hostelry, and this had to be remedied by the conversion of an ordinary dwelling a few yards from the railway line in the hamlet of Ireland, later known as the Black Horse. During the summer of 1854 the labour force was reduced by a quarter when men returned to harvest fields in their own villages.

Accidents during the construction of the line were not frequent, but those that did occur were often fatal. On 12 February 1855 a group of men were working on the excavation of a cutting near Southill when it collapsed and buried two of them, one dying within an hour of being dug out. Three weeks later at the north end of the Warden tunnel an embankment caved in and buried a labourer, Charles Clarke. The earth was quickly removed, but he died soon afterwards.

Eventually the line was completed on 8 April 1857. Brassey had built 63 miles of track for £1,000,000. To reduce costs the contours of the land had been followed as closely as possible. Liddell was frustrated by the technical limitations that this imposed. Beyond Bedford, as one passed into Whitbread's territory, there was a steep ascent from Cardington to Warden tunnel. At a later date locomotives of goods trains were reduced to walking pace as they entered the 880 yard structure, built by John Knowles of Shefford. If the wind was blowing from the northwest the smoke would fill the driver's cab, and one driver reported that the only way to breathe was to get down on to the lowest step at the side of the engine and let the locomotive take the train through. The footplate was resumed at the end of the tunnel. Luckily Warden tunnel was dry. If it had been wet the engine

Southill Railway Station in January 1969

wheels would have slipped, and the crew would have had to stay on the footplate.

The stations at Southill and Cardington conformed to a standard design. The platforms were rather low, presumably for economy, and the buildings were relatively small, of yellow brick and with lozenge type windows set in cast iron frames. The station at Southill had been begun in February 1856, but work was slow due to a shortage of bricks. The Midland sought to man the stations with courteous and helpful staff, anxious to maintain the good reputation of the company. At Cardington station there was a porter, signalman and station master. Each station had cattle and sheep pens and, most important, a coal yard. Carriers were later to call daily to convey heavy goods to the villages on the estate. Cheaper coal was a direct result of the coming of the railway.

The line was opened on Thursday 7 May 1857. The day was declared a public holiday in Bedford, and the first excursion left Hitchin at 7.30 am, calling at Southill at 8.15 am and Bedford at 9 am before travelling on to Leicester, arriving at 12 noon. *The Bedford Times* reported that in Bedford shops were closed and streamers waved from buildings in different parts of the town. Crowds of people flocked to the railway station, which was still the London and North Western Station at St John's, to secure their places several hours in advance. The Mayor and Corporation assembled at the Shire Hall and walked in procession to the station, preceded by the band of the Bedfordshire Militia. They boarded the train to Leicester where they were met by the Chairman and Directors of the Midland Railway. Returning in the afternoon, the Mayor presided at a dinner at the Bedford Rooms in the evening. There is no mention of William Henry at the dinner, but his brother Samuel Charles Whitbread was there. The passenger service proper commenced the following day when 18 carriages left Hitchin station at 7.33 am. The fare from Hitchin to Leicester was first class 4s, second class 2s, and third class 1s.

When passengers wanted to travel to London they had to change at Hitchin on to Great Northern trains, and the Midland paid £500 rent for these facilities. The arrangement lasted for less than a year, and from 1 February 1858 Midland trains ran over the Great Northern rails to Kings Cross. For this privilege the Midland was charged £60,000 annually. From 1 February 1859 passengers were able to use the new Bedford station north of the river, known as Midland Road.

For William Henry Whitbread, his vision had been realised. A vital link from the midlands to London had been routed through the Southill Estate. He had negotiated with the Board the right to stop trains at Southill and Cardington, to ensure that the estate's best interests were served. Since not all trains stopped at these stations he introduced various methods to make sure that his rights were not forgotten. Game keepers on the estate would be told to tackle the station masters and ask them to stop trains so that animals could be placed in the guards' vans at Cardington and taken off at Southill, or vice versa. This often irritated the punctilious railway staff, but Whitbread was insistent.

The September 1860 timetable was printed in *The Bedfordshire Mercury* and showed that five trains on weekdays passed through Southill in each direction and two on Sundays. The midafternoon and late evening trains did not stop at Cardington and Southill unless Whitbread intervened. The lunchtime and early evening trains carried all three fare classes, promoting relatively cheap travel. An example of costs is shown by an excursion on Tuesday 11 September 1860 to a Horticultural and Floral Fête and Balloon Ascent at Wellingborough. The return fare was 1s 6d from Southill and 1s from Cardington.

Whitbread allowed his park to be used for special excursions coming by rail. For example, on Friday 21 June 1861 several corps of rifle volunteers assembled there. *The Bedfordshire Mercury* reported that the men had left the Midland Road station at 2.25 pm. Unfortunately, heavy rain continued throughout the afternoon. This did not appear to dampen their spirits and after refreshments, they gave Mr Whitbread three cheers. Accompanying bands then struck up and the men marched back to Southill station. The largest occasion which Whitbread supported was on 17 July 1866 when a great fête was held at Southill and 2,000 passengers travelled from Bedford station.

The safety record on the line at this time appears to be good, but one accident brought home the potential dangers. In April 1865 a pick-up goods train stopped at Southill on its way to King's Cross. Thomas Charlton, the guard, informed William Oldham, the driver, that whilst shunting they were to drop off one waggon and pick up four. After safely completing the first operation, Charlton went forward to hook on the extra waggons. He tripped and was crushed by the buffers. The inquest was held at the White Horse public house and a verdict of accidental death was returned by Mr Whyley, the coroner.

On a bleak January day in 1867 Charles Dickens passed through Southill on the stopping train to Hitchin. He had rested for a while in Bedford due to "the reckless fury of the driving" of the fast train from Leicester.

William Henry Whitbread died on Friday 21 June 1867. His funeral was the following Thursday. The cortège left the house at 9.00 am for Cardington church and the family vault. Appropriately, the family and mourners were met outside Southill station by many other relatives and supporters who had arrived by train from London, and the procession paused there before proceeding to Cardington. In 1864 an obelisk had been erected in public gratitude to William Henry

Obelisk in Keepers' Warren, Southill, to William Henry Whitbread, 1864

Whitbread's liberality as a supporter of railways. It stands on estate land close to Southill Station, and could be seen from the train as it left for Shefford. It is inscribed:

To William Henry Whitbread Esq. for his zeal and energy in promoting railways through the County of Bedford. 1864. Erected by public subscription.

As the inscription suggests, the Midland railway through Southill was not his only contribution. As early as 1840 he is reported as supporting the formation of the Bedford Railway Company: "Mr Whitbread advocates it most strenuously and will offer every support he can to it". In 1845 he was writing to the Board of Trade to help the Great Northern Railway. In 1860 he was at the Great Northern Hotel in London to give his support to the Luton Dunstable and Welwyn Junction Railway. His most distinguished contribution was as Chairman of the Board of the Bedford and Northampton Railway from 1864. At the banquet to celebrate its opening on 26 July 1872 Colonel Higgins spoke warmly of Whitbread, "lamenting that he could not have lived to see the accomplishment of the object he had so much at heart".

His death in 1867 prevented him from seeing the tragedy which befell his own particular line through Southill, one which he must have foreseen. Owing to the amount of traffic there occurred a breakdown in the relations between the Midland and the Great Northern over congestion on the track from Hitchin to London. This had come to a crisis during the trade exhibition in London in 1862 and after a serious accident in a tunnel at Welwyn in 1866. The result was that the Midland decided to build its own line to London, and in 1868 the direct line from Bedford to St Pancras was finished. As a result, the Bedford to Hitchin route was reduced to a branch line.

It was left to William Henry's brother, Samuel Charles Whitbread to keep up the fight for the stopping of trains at Southill and Cardington so that the estate might continue to benefit. He was in regular correspondence with James Allport, Midland Chairman from 1853 to 1857 and again from 1860 to 1880. In one such letter of 5 October 1870 Allport reminds Whitbread that he had written after the opening of the Bedford to St Pancras line to explain why it was necessary to change the line to branch status, which Whitbread had taken exception to, and confirms that he had not ignored the wants of the district. He also draws to Whitbread's attention that he appeared to be somewhat mistaken as to the terms of the arrangement with regard to stopping trains at Southill and Cardington. Allport states:

"the deed to which you refer provides that you shall be at liberty to stop at Southill any train you require for your accommodation; but as regards Cardington, the number of trains to stop there are limited to two up and two down trains, and as you are aware, more than that number daily call at that place. I feel that I have only to point this out to you, to reverse the impression which I think you must have been under, when you gave orders to the station master at Southill to stop the 9.38 am train at Cardington on the 13th ultimo."

Samuel Charles continued to welcome excursions to Southill Park. *The Bedfordshire Mercury* reported that on 18 August 1868 the teachers of the Bunyan Meeting Sunday School and a few friends, numbering 53, proceeded by the 11.58 train from Bedford to Southill station, tickets having been issued at single 2nd class fare for the double journey. The party entered the park and were conducted through the beautiful gardens. Tea was prepared on the banks of the lake after which the party enjoyed "innocent games" before strolling to Warden church. They returned on the 7.39 train to Bedford "having enjoyed the rural picnic exceedingly".

It is clear that the reduction in status of the Bedford to Hitchin line meant that the Whitbread family used its service less frequently. In the early 1890s Samuel Charles' son, Samuel Whitbread, who was MP for Bedford, was reported as regularly catching the express at Biggleswade to travel to the House of Commons. He was delivered by trap from Southill and collected in the evening. The trap also picked up the cook's fish at the station. It came from Grimsby every morning by fast train on the Great Northern, and had to be collected immediately so as to remain fresh.

The Whitbread family at this time moved to London for the opening of Parliament. For some days prior to their departure a train would be in the bay of the station for parcels and luggage to be taken down, as well as provisions, laundry bags, baskets, etc.. When the time came Mr Whitbread and his wife travelled in a first class carriage at the front, maidservants in their own carriage, as were the menservants, coachmen and grooms, and at the end a number of horses in the guard's van. Their destination has been reported as St Pancras, so presumably the Midland line from Bedford was used.

Each station on the Midland Railway operated a claims register and the station master was authorised to settle small claims without reference to headquarters. Up to 1922 the limit was £5. A country station like Southill would be involved chiefly in claims by farmers or merchants for goods damaged in transit. On the 28 February 1920 £2 14s was claimed for the loss of four bottles of whisky. In 1926 Samuel Howard Whitbread recorded a public complaint over the delay in delivering a load of tarred limestone.

Horace Mann, a fireman on the Midland Railway from 1922, has recalled one incident on the line which took place on a winter's night in the 1920s when he was working on the late train from Hitchin to Bedford. The train had stopped at Henlow and was just pulling out when he noticed a girl fall between the footboard and the platform as she tried to enter the moving train. Unfortunately she became wedged between the coach and platform. He uncoupled the coach and with a pinch bar moved it slowly back. The girl was freed and laid on cushions. The station master at Shefford called Bedford for an ambulance and the staff at Southill and Cardington stations reported that they had no passengers waiting for the train. Consequently the girl was able to be rushed to Bedford non-stop and her life was saved.

During the two World Wars the railway line took on a particular significance.

In the first war German prisoners were held in a camp close to Southill station and were brought there to work on local farms. In the second, the Home Guard sited their shooting range on the estate opposite the Black Horse public house in Ireland, close to the railway. They had to patrol from Southill station through the Warden Tunnel, which had been the subject of incendiary devices. It was believed that ammunition was stored there, and certainly Southill was used to transfer ammunition in and out of a local depot in Park Wood on the Shuttleworth Estate. Between these two places was constructed a new track, where a diesel engine supplied the three loading bays.

The original double track from Bedford to Hitchin had been singled in 1912, except between Southill and Shefford, and shortly thereafter the Sunday service disappeared. The advent of buses in rural areas in the 1920s contributed to the decline in passengers, and the growth of motor transport sealed the line's fate. There continued to be a service of steam 'rail motor' trains until 1960, when diesel multiple units and unusual four wheeled rail buses ran, the latter put on by British Railways to stimulate travel. Seven trains ran each way daily, except Sundays, but they failed to restore popular demand for the line. Inevitably, the line was selected for closure by the British Transport Commission, and the last scheduled passenger train between Cardington and Henlow was in 1962.

The track was not taken up until the end of 1964 and so it was still available in the May of that year for the filming of *Those Magnificent Men in their Flying Machines*. A train was recorded travelling from Cardington to Southill and making the climb to Warden Tunnel, disguised as if to resemble the Nord Railway of France. The actor Terry Thomas was shown in a triplane as if he had landed it on the roof of the train. When the train emerged at the end of the tunnel the wings of the plane appeared to have been torn off, a humorous incident with which to end Southill's association with the railway age.

Chapter 9

Southill at War

by CAROL PERRY

AT THE OUTBREAK of the First World War, Madeline Whitbread threw herself into the war effort as President of the Soldiers' and Sailors' Families Association. In a letter to the editor of The Biggleswade Chronicle in August 1914 she wrote "The men are doing their part. Ours is to see that the homes of the families they have left behind are maintained in their absence". Mrs Whitbread was subsequently nominated chairman of the Women's War Agricultural Committee, responsible for getting women to work on the land to replace the men at the front.

The villagers on the estate and surrounding area gave what they could for the war effort. Vegetables for the Navy were collected weekly from designated farms and collections were taken at church for the purchase of parcels for Bedfordshire prisoners of war in Germany. Soldiers were stationed all around the area. In January 1915 the military took over the Assembly Hall in Broom in order to billet soldiers there before they went to the front and from May 1916 the land known as Upper and Lower Seacots within Southill Park was let to the Government for use as a military camp. Military exercises took place in the villages, particularly line laying. Lines for communication purposes would be laid out and then later reeled in as practice for the trenches.

The influx of soldiers into the area was not without incident. In June 1916 a young private, Joseph Potts of the 2/7th Cheshire Regiment from the West Brigade Camp at Old Warden, was drowned whilst bathing in Southill Lake. Owing to the depth of the water and the quantity of weeds the body was not recovered until the following day. He was buried with full military honours at St Leonard's church, Old Warden.

Samuel Whitbread offered some of the newly built estate cottages at Broom Cross Roads to Belgian refugees and a committee was formed in Southill to help provide financial support for them. The Van Damm family were one of those to move in. Mr Van Damm had been a cabinet maker in Belgium and found work at John King's farm at Broom. The children went to school at Southill. The headmaster at that time was Mr J B Jones, a Welshman who was considered to be very strict but fair. He took a particular interest in the boys, who were each given a garden plot to work on two afternoons a week. The young gardeners sent large quantities of vegetables to Naval bases such as Gorleston, and to sailors based at Aberdeen. The boys also used to go to the elderly and widows and dig their gardens for them. Bill Camp particularly remembers going with other boys to the cottages at Gastlings and digging potatoes and then lighting a fire and baking some as a reward for their hard work. As a result of this, Mr Jones was flooded with requests from women who also wanted their gardens dug!! While the boys were gardening, the girls made garments for the soldiers – socks, belts, scarves and gloves.

The early months of 1916 saw some very harsh weather conditions. On 28 March 1916 there was a terrible blizzard which lasted from three in the afternoon until midnight. The roads were impassable the next morning – there were snow drifts four or five feet deep and hundreds of trees were brought down, many of them lying where they had fallen for years afterwards. The night before the blizzard a dispatch rider was forced to abandon his motor cycle at Shefford because of the snow. He walked to Broom Cross Roads and collapsed outside the estate cottages just as Bill Camp's father was going out to visit the Van Damm family, who lived next door. Mr Camp brought the man in and he slept in Bill's bed that night, walking on to his depot in Biggleswade the next day.

German prisoners of war were based near Southill Station, and they were set to work on the local farms. By June 1919 gangs of prisoners were working at Clifton Bury, Shillington, Meppershall and Broom. They had a cottage in Broom which they called "Frau Catti abode" and went there to brew cups of tea. They were extremely hard working and required very little supervision – Frank Perridge, whose father ran the sawmills, occasionally kept sole guard over the prisoners while they were felling trees.

Letters from the men at the front were printed in *The Biggleswade Chronicle*. In June 1916 Fred Ballard was able to write home with a graphic account of life in the trenches. "For the past three weeks a part of our regiment has been doing trench work in a very hot part of the line. You will be very pleased to learn that several Southill boys are with this party viz. C Lockey, Sid Hall and George Bean; this is a fine experience for all of us. We are billeted in a village, or rather the remains of one, as everything is in a terrible state of ruin. The Sunday night we came into the place the Boches attacked and got into our front trenches, but were driven out by the brigade bombers; we were told that Fritz sent no less than half a million shells over our lines in four and a half hours, so we evacuated our front line trench as it was no use. The next two nights the laugh was on our side, our artillery bombarding their trenches all night long; since then things have been much quieter. Really it does not seem possible for humanity to live in such affairs as these with so many pieces of spare iron flying about."

Many of the men never came back and those who did often had harrowing stories to tell. Lance Corporal Herbert Hall arrived back home in Southill in December 1918, having been a prisoner of war in Germany. Many of his comrades had been killed by British gunfire and food had been in very short supply, the men catching snails and frogs to eat when they got a chance. Herbert had never received a parcel or any of the letters that had been sent to him.

The end of the war was marked by tragedies at home, when an influenza epidemic swept through the area. At least eight of the prisoners of war held near Southill Station died of influenza. Whole families were ill at the same time and Southill School was forced to close for a month. Florence Jones, the elder daughter of Mr Jones, the headmaster, died in the epidemic. Her fiancé, Fred Ballard, was one of those chosen to march to the Rhine, and so was not able to get home for her funeral, and neither could many of her relatives get to Southill, because of the poor postal and rail communications.

In July 1919 a special peace day celebration was held at Southill Park to which all the local children were invited. A marquee was erected on the lawn and a large tea was provided followed by games under cover, as the weather was unsettled. Mrs Whitbread presented every child with a Peace Medal and the afternoon finished with a grand procession of decorated motors, cycles, bath chairs, hand trucks and fancy costumes, all headed by a jazz band.

The men arriving home from the war faced a housing shortage – there had been little building during the war years. The 1919 Housing and Town Planning Act imposed a duty on local authorities to provide homes, and this led to the building of many council houses in the villages. In March 1920, the Housing Committee of Biggleswade Rural District Council proposed 30 houses for Broom, 5 for Stanford Road in Southill, and 10 for Stanford. A livelihood for many of the returning soldiers was provided by smallholdings. The Whitbread Estate had leased some land to the Bedfordshire County Council for smallholdings before the war. When the war ended, further land such as Broom Farm was leased so as to help the returning soldiers. The land was good market gardening land, and crops were grown for the London markets, going up regularly by lorry, until the bombing in the Second World War made this impracticable. After the war in 1919 a branch of the Women's Institute was founded in Southill under the presidency of Mrs

Whitbread, and as in other places this helped to bring new ideas to the village.

During the Second World War the Royal Army Ordnance Corps, 27 ASD took over much of the Whitbread and Shuttleworth estates. They built a camp at Gastlings and used part of Southill House as an officers' mess. A small contingent of Military Police was housed at Home Farm. The railheads at Sandy, Biggleswade, Southill and Shefford were used for moving ammunition. The camp consisted of a few hundred personnel and also a labour force, initially the Pioneer Corps and later Italian and German prisoners of war. The whole area became one huge ammunition dump, with galvanised huts full of ammunition all around the roads of Southill and beyond; though most of the ammunition was stored in the woods on the Shuttleworth estate. The RAOC camp built up its own community, using whatever talent there was. The camp had its own tailor, shoemaker, barber, cricket club and even its own dance band.

The villagers quickly became involved in war work of one kind or another, be it in the A R P or Home Guard, as Special Constables, Fire Watchers or the Red Cross. Sewing parties took place at Southill House to provide comforts for the troops, and local women also took their turn helping at the soldiers' canteen in a barn at Gastlings.

Being in the country, rationing was supplemented by local supplies. Mrs Faulkener in Southill borrowed canning machines and peaches were canned at her premises for local use. Farmworkers were allowed extra cheese rations because of the nature of their work and people managed to get by with a little trading here and there.

Southill school and the Clubroom at Southill House were used for social functions. Dances for the comforts fund were held weekly – three dances on a small scale in the Clubroom and a larger dance once a month at the school. The functions at the school made a lot of work. All the desks had to be cleared and, if there was to be ballroom dancing, the floor had to be chalked. A farmer's stack sheet was placed against the windows to provide a black out and a piano was brought in. The organisers started work at four thirty in the afternoon, and it was often half past one in the morning by the time all had been cleared up and put back. After the war the villagers formed a committee to provide their own village hall, and obtained a hut from Henlow Camp which had originally been a .22 rifle range.

Meetings of the Southill Home Guard were held at the school, and there was a shooting range opposite the Black Horse pub at Ireland. Bill Camp remembers his first attempts at shooting. "The sergeant gave me instructions how to operate the gun and there was half a dozen of us new recruits who had to lay down and take our first shot. I was the first one on the mat and the officer Lt. Linford (head keeper on the Whitbread Estate) gave the order to fire. I pulled my trigger, fired and they waved back from the pit what you'd done. Linford said 'Excellent shot, Camp, good, straight up six o'clock'. That meant you'd fired straight in line. He claimed that was an excellent shot. After that I did become quite a good shot".

An old shepherd's hut was used by those members who were on duty at night, and the local policeman, Bernard Sparrow, used to come back from police meetings at Biggleswade and terrify the men and boys on duty with stories about the fifth column – how infiltrators were landing in Britain, getting information and sending it back to Germany.

The Home Guard also had to patrol Southill Station at nights, right through to the Bedford end of the long tunnel. This was not always done properly as Bill Clark remembers. "To prove the Southill side had walked the tunnel you had to take a pair of plimsols through to prove that you had been there – one this end, one the other. Some bright spark bought a pair the same. Nobody walked the tunnel!".

Red Cross meetings were held at the Clubroom at Southill House. From October 1940 until the end of the war, Old Warden Park was used as a convalescent home for troops and the local Red Cross nurses went at weekends to relieve the regular staff. Before they commenced their duties of handing round tea, washing bandages and pushing men round the grounds, they had to face an inspection by the Red Cross Commandant, Mrs Shuttleworth, who was considered to be quite a fearsome lady. The Red Cross nurses were also involved in the local Home Guard exercises. At one of these the 'enemy' managed to get into the park with a car and threw smoke bombs at the defenders, causing injury to some of them. Unfortunately the nurses did not realise this, and when the casualties came in semi-conscious on stretchers, the nurses thought that these were just excellent actors. Dr Irish, the Shefford doctor, came in and had a look at them and, realising that they were in fact real casualties, sent them straight to hospital.

The hazard of having a large amount of ammunition stored in the area meant that at the beginning of the war Southill had its own fire service. Southill Fire Service consisted of three men, Len Hall, Len's father and Bert Pierce. The men enrolled at Biggleswade fire station and were supplied with a hose pipe and a stand for getting the water out. Originally the transport for the equipment was a wheel barrow! Nine pounds was raised by means of a raffle and a little old Morris Minor car was bought to carry the equipment, Len Hall himself putting in the extra pound needed to cover the cost. The fire service lasted for about a couple of years and was then disbanded, as there were now extra men to cover the area at Biggleswade and Shefford.

Shortly after the outbreak of war, evacuees began to arrive from London. Phyllis Clark remembers the children arriving at Southill in a double decker bus, hanging out of the windows and shouting. They were taken to the School and then billeted out. An attempt was made to try to keep families together, but it took some time for everything to be sorted out. At first the children wandered round looking lost – they were shocked more by the silence than by bombs – but soon they made the village come alive with their presence. By September 1939 Southill School had increased the number of children on its register from 70 to 160. More children arrived at the beginning of October 1939 and the Assembly Rooms at Broom were used as an additional school building. Not many stayed on after the war, the majority gradually filtering back to where they had come from.

Since 1928 the Queen's brother, the Hon Michael Bowes-Lyon, had lived with his family at Gastlings on the Whitbread Estate. During the Second World War Michael Bowes-Lyon became the commander of the 2nd Battalion Bedfordshire Home Guard. The headquarters had originally been at the Estate

The Queen (now the Queen Mother) inspecting Southill Red Cross in 1943 at "Gastlings", the home of Col. Bowes-Lyon – brother of the Queen Mother

Office at Southill, but later moved to Biggleswade. In July 1944 the Queen visited Biggleswade to inspect her brother's battalion. The tour began at Fairfield where the Home Guard were lined up waiting to be inspected (having waited a good half an hour as the Queen was late) and then moved on to Broom and Southill. At Broom Hall several members of the Women's Land Army stood to attention. Flags flew everywhere and practically the whole village turned out for the occasion. At Southill flags and bunting were displayed, and a large union flag was hung over the entrance to Southill House. The 18th Beds (Southill) Detachment of Red Cross nurses commanded by the Hon Mrs Elizabeth Bowes-Lyon were waiting for the Queen's arrival at Gastlings. The Queen walked slowly between the ranks and spoke to several of the nurses before going into the house to stay with her relatives.

There was very little enemy damage in the area which was fortunate, considering that ammunition was stored everywhere. A bomb was dropped at Broom Cross Roads in October 1940 and bombs were also dropped at Haynes turn, the

Repairing the road at Broom Crossroads – a bomb crater, 1940

pilot perhaps mistaking the shape of the trees there for the hangars at Cardington. The Gilberts at Park Farm, Old Warden, received a shock in the early hours of a Saturday morning in August 1944. A Mosquito from Graveley Station crashed into the farm house, killing the pilot and navigator. Serious damage was done to the dairy as well as other buildings. Mrs Gilbert and her daughter Kathleen, who were both asleep, had remarkable escapes. A propeller crashed its way right through the room, taking with it the spring mattress and parts of the bed. Mrs Gilbert suffered shock and lacerations but both she and her daughter escaped serious injury. Equally fortunate was an Italian prisoner of war who was sleeping in the bedroom above the kitchen. A length of tubing weighing several pounds fell on his pillow, narrowly missing his head. The engines of the plane were later found between five and six hundred yards behind the dairy.

Special parties were held in the villages to celebrate V E and V J days. Southill school was closed for the day on 30 May 1945 so that the children could attend

VE Day party in Southill School, 1945

a sports meeting at Southill Park followed by tea at the school. All the children of Broom under the age of 16 and the Old Age Pensioners were given a victory tea for V J day in August 1945. This was followed by a huge bonfire on the green and a Victory party at Broom Assembly Room. The bonfires were particularly special as they had been banned during the war. Gradually men who had been held prisoners of war by the Japanese came home, and an official reception for them was held at Biggleswade on 12 January 1946 organised under the presidency of Admiral Sir Lionel Halsey.

Despite the jubilation and the tremendous sense of relief at the end of the war, Britain was to endure more years of rationing and "make do and mend". Phyllis and Bill Clark were married at Southill Church on 1 July 1944. The church bells in Southill were allowed to be rung for the first time since the outbreak of war. Until then, church bells could only be rung in the event of an invasion. For the Clarks, setting up home was not an easy matter. At the end of the Second World War as at the end of the First, there was a great shortage of housing, and the Clarks were unable to get a house of their own and so they lived with Phyllis' mother. Dockets were issued for furniture and they were allowed enough dockets to buy a bed, a wardrobe and a dressing table, though they didn't have enough for a table and chairs. Once a couple had been married a certain time they were allowed more furniture, and the Clarks subsequently bought a three piece suite. All their furniture was bought from a firm at Shuttleworth Aerodrome, which made the best utility furniture in the area.

One of the very best treats for Phyllis Clark after the war had ended was a trip on a bus to the sea. The war had been on during the whole of her teenage years and travel to the seaside had been impossible. The end of the war meant that old freedoms could now be taken for granted and gradually life could return to normal.

Chapter 10

Southill Estate Buildings – an Architectural Tour

by BERNARD WEST

ANY REVIEW OF the Whitbread years must include the involvement of the family with the maintenance of those churches of medieval foundation on the estate. In the country as a whole, the two hundred years from 1795 to 1995 (in the earlier years at least) were not the ideal time for the conservation of surviving medieval buildings. Southill, Elstow and Cardington perfectly illustrate the three main categories into which the loss of authenticity could fall, through so-called restoration of one kind or another. However, this is not to say that this always involved the automatic loss of character or identity.

Southill church acquired its present appearance at a time "a little too late for Gothic romance, and a little too early for archaeological accuracy". At Elstow archaeological assurance, combined with arrogance, replaced, scraped and trivialised the church; whereas at Cardington, a late and totally unnecessary rebuilding transformed it.

Southill church in 1811 must have been near dereliction when George Cloake prepared the original scheme for its restoration. He died however in 1812 and his specification was revised and resubmitted for approval by S W Reynolds, largely in accordance with Cloake's original intentions. The actual contract was undertaken by Thomas Martin. Essentially the core of the building – nave arcades and clerestory – is a rebuilding of this time, with the aisles retaining much of their medieval character. As it happens this is the most attractive interior of the three, quiet and dignified with some beautiful texture, particularly in the brick flooring. Genuinely medieval, the north west window of the north aisle, with beautiful tracery of Kentish type, must be c. 1300, and one is perhaps ungenerously amazed that Reynolds never tampered with it in his rebuilding.

At St Mary and St Helena, Elstow, Thomas Jobson Jackson's 'restoration' was full blooded to the point of heartlessness. Watercolours of the interior in 1830

Workmen employed on the rebuilding of Elstow Church, 1880-2

show what has been lost, a decent plastered interior; and others of the work in progress are more a record of demolition. The detail was accurate enough as far as one can make out from old engravings, but with more alterations than could be justified. For example the original, high square-headed windows of the south aisle, raised to accommodate the cloister roof, were replaced by lower two-centred arched substitutes, thus destroying the evidence of an original monastic character.

How much all of this accorded with the wishes of Samuel Whitbread III (1830-1915) it is hard to say, but one has a feeling that with Jackson in charge, or more probably, his foreman, everything that could be replaced or retooled was in fact given the full treatment. The ex Norman north door, formerly in an attractive timber porch, is the saddest thing, now a piece of machine-made vulgarity more appropriate to St Cuthbert's in Bedford, or some North London suburb. The interior has been made to look naive, though the original grandeur to some extent survives. We have here a scraped and stripped treatment, followed by particularly tedious tuck pointing. Always a nasty treatment of masonry, at least it is not in red mortar, like the ghastly reticulation at St Peter's, Bedford.

Elstow Church restoration, by Thomas Jobson Jackson, 1880

At Cardington, one finds a grand interior, almost Cistercian in its austerity. Only in the surviving chancel of the old church with its Gascoigne and Harvey tombs is there any degree of richness. The Wedgwood black basalt ware font, given to the church by Harriot Whitbread in 1783 is deservedly famous, matched only by its twin at Essendon in Hertfordshire. One wonders when and how a third disappeared from Melchbourne, a strange thing to steal and even stranger to destroy. In the north transept, the monument to Samuel Charles Whitbread of 1879 is by Weekes, and a distinguished piece of sculpture, with husband and wife kneeling tenderly together. Peter Scheemakers did the monument to Ive Whitbread sometime after 1766 in the form of two impressive busts. That to Samuel Whitbread I of 1796 is in the Grecian mode of the time, and shows him somewhat incongruously half clothed on a couch. All this is by John Bacon who is normally lacking in emotion which is not the case here, in fact rather the reverse, hence one's comments on incongruity. Weekes' monument to Samuel Whitbread II of 1849 is a sound piece of work in both archaeological and artistic terms. In the south chapel is fixed the poignant memorial of 1791 to William Charles Whitbread, a small child.

Cardington Church before rebuilding began in 1897

Across the road is Albert Richardson's monument to those killed in the R101 airship disaster of 1930. One always remembers him saying that the most moving form of memorial is one on which you look down, which is the form here. Oddly, the opposite to the way in which Lutyens would have designed it.

The fabric of the church is an alien sandstone from Derbyshire, of an unfortunate and vaguely fleshy colour, which seems to have been used as random rubble for housing on the Green at numbers 322/3 and also round the corner at Southill Road numbers 285/7, near the old Exeter Arms. The style is late Perpendicular, accurate enough, but mechanical, and there is an unhappy separation in the belfry lights in the tower, by a panel with cusped heads which has few medieval precedents. The architect George Highton used estate labour for the rebuilding, but no doubt architectural elements, window tracery and mouldings to reveals, were shopwork production. With their too perfect crispness they look it, and only long term weathering can soften the outlines.

Building in the estate villages was set in the context of limited late medieval survivals, such as Elstow High Street for example, or in more substantial yeoman housing of the 16th to 18th centuries, preceding the Whitbread years. Initially this involved replacement and infilling in a restrained late Georgian tradition, continuing the practice of the Torrington management. Some of the earlier cottages, one or two now sadly derelict, carry the characteristic, and most attractive, initial and date roundels, although one of the prettiest, 'The Cottage', on Cardington Green of 1764, dates from earlier, albeit restored by the Whitbreads.

Various individual buildings on the estate deserve a mention, whether wholly dating from the Whitbread years or not; lovely houses like the farm at Herrings' Green, a double pile Georgian house now sadly lacking the monumental elms which used to set it off. In the park itself there are such hidden delights as Gastlings, once a country house with Bowes-Lyon associations, and thus with our present Queen Mother. This is an E plan house presumably of the late 17th century to which two bays have been added c.1790-1800 in the same general style. The whole range is now newly rendered in the traditional pale ochre colour wash. Adjoining outbuildings make a lovely composition worthy of Crome or Cotman in their picturesqueness.

Park Farm is a most unlikely building with an east elevation which sprouts an ambitious classical porch, and complex glazed door surround. It has a fluted cornice which extends across the whole east front. At the north end is the old tiled dairy with a big semi-circular headed window on the north gable. The farm is still known as the Tent House, and tradition has it that an internal silk marquee was slung inside the original structure, with the house silver brought over for picnics and parties. A maze in the garden, long since gone, was part of the entertainment. In the farmyard is a delightful octagonal grain store on eight staddle stones against rodent attack. Weatherboarded with a tiled roof, this is the perfect example of the fitness for purpose of a truly functional building.

Glebe House to the north of the church is a classic piece of 18th century eclecticism, Venetian windows, lunette window and verandah, which cuts the head of the entrance door somewhat brutally. It is a lively composition derived directly from pattern books, with more enthusiasm than scholarship.

Southill is of course the heartland of the estate and the High Street is a delight from end to end; not in any way selfconsciously romantic, as is Old Warden, but of a genuinely village character. Gracious Farm and its outbuildings to the east of the excellent White Horse, no longer in estate ownership, is a fine group. The house itself with a remarkable though mutilated fireplace inside, dating from the late sixteenth century, has been sold, and the new farmhouse to the east, double-gabled like the old house, is a somewhat selfconscious piece of neo-vernacular, where the hand of the Planners' intervention is only too obvious.

Numbers 33 to 36 built in a very pretty pale gault brick, so pale they are probably not Arlesey bricks, but Burwells with excellent chamfered red rubbed brick to window heads and reveals, and red brick quoining also to all external angles. The coupled arches in the centre of the composition, numbers 34 and 35, are not helped by the insertion of rather mean doors, replacing the original open porches. With its dense pattern of cast iron diamond pane glazing, hell to clean, one would imagine, this is a memorable range of buildings. Of 1874, like number 39, this is of the era of Samuel Whitbread III. He it was who couldn't read working drawings, and had models made, particularly of later work towards the turn of the century. Nevertheless there is evidence that he may have been the amateur architect of a lot of the work on the estate in a sort of sub-Jacobean style. The models are a feature of the Estate Office, used for book ends, paper weights etc., but are perhaps worthy of better display.

Numbers 43-46 repeat 33-36 but with slightly less style. Was this by any chance the work of another contractor, or less competent estate workers? Numbers 56-59 opposite are intriguing, apparently late Georgian with a third floor in a mansard roof. The glazing in lead cames, set in heavy iron frames, gives a very early appearance to the fenestration, more in accordance with William and Mary of, say, 1690-1700, which is unlikely. Numbers 52-59 were known locally as The Poor's House. More research on this range would be worth while.

Number 52 is Southill Stores, a village shop mercifully still surviving. This is a very pretty group, with a shallow, very refined hood and door case to the adjoining cottage. Dated 'S.W. 1815', this was the year of Samuel II's death. Number 39 of 1874 has a severe long gault brick elevation, with chamfered segmental arched windows, and cast iron glazing bars. These have most attractive cusped arched heads of a vaguely Gothic flavour, in each bay of 3 lights. The ogee lead roof on delicate trellis is near to the Chinese taste of the time, and very sophisticated. Hidden by high hedging this is a building of severe but immense character.

Numbers 63 and 64 opposite number 32, are a cottage interlude, probably late 18th century, and fairly certainly pre-Whitbread, maybe Torrington. They are thatched and colour washed and very picturesque. 66, 67 and 68 with two gable ends to the street, the centre parallel to it, looks very much as if it is an older structure, with the same diamond panes as numbers 34 and 35, and with elaborate barge boards. Two chimney stacks give the impression that this is actually a late 17th century yeoman's house, but given the estate treatment under Samuel Charles in the 1870s.

Finally one must comment on Howard Close of 1983 by John Manning, a

25-26 School Lane, Southill, by Bernard West

picturesque contemporary interpretation of the *genius loci*, the whole design being unified by a loggia or verandah treatment. Pastiche is carefully avoided, but more care of the immediate landscape would be welcome.

There is so much to detain one in the village that full descriptions could become a tedious list. The Baptist Chapel has a memorable interior but is not a part of the estate. However, we cannot leave without considering the most attractive School Lane. Southill Lower School is unique: a 'cat and kittens' combination of a somewhat gargantuan gault brick extension to the older thatched wing, cottage ornée with elongated honeycomb fenestration in lead cames, and with the usual decent paling fence along the road frontage.

Stanford, dominated by Village Farm to the south east, has another typical range in the sub-Jacobean style, characteristic of Samuel III's work on the estate. This is of 1901 and features the use of gritstone window lintels. This occurs earlier in a remote setting, the last house down Mill Lane before the river. It is of 1892 and is set in a strangely remote landscape considering the surrounding intensive agriculture. The river here is not as intriguing as a map would suggest, the Ivel Navigation channel having taken most of the water away from the old course.

The low cost housing in The Crescent unfortunately advertises its status. Dreadfully thin detailing to the gables, which would have benefited from the use of bargeboards, gives the whole a rather pinched look, worthy, but a little inadequate.

At Broom there is a remarkable Germanic range of housing, numbers 37 to 44. Is this due to the swastika glazing in the heads of the ground floor windows, or the succession of hips and gables that would not look out of place in Nuremburg? It is all impressive but rather forbidding.

Elstow retains a scattering of estate properties, the best range being in West End Lane. Dating from 1903 to 1908, they have grand chimney stacks with reconstituted stone caps, pebble dashed upper floors; and the usual verandah style roof between gable ends. Today they form a bastion of the old village against a rising tide of suburban neo-vernacular that threatens them from the north.

The long eastern side of the High Street south of the Nursery, was sold to the old Bedford Rural District Council in the 1970s, and the writer had the great good fortune to be retained to carry out the restoration, conversion and infill of the entire street and its hinterland. Later infilling has been carried out by the Bedford Borough Council. Some of this range contains very early timber construction indeed, as early as the 13th century, but a detailed architectural record of the work and its restoration would justify a separate study and is really beyond the remit of this article. Opposite, hugging the Swan public house, is Mr Prudden's cottage, its jettied frontage indicating a late medieval date. This is the one house in the village awaiting restoration. If as one imagines there is a pattern of closely spaced timbers behind the rendering of the first floor, one could probably date it to the late fourteen hundreds. The battlemented beam of the oversail could justify such a conclusion.

Elstow Lodge, south of the brook, has the Hampstead look characteristic of 1930s neo-Georgian, but it makes no major contribution to the street scene. Village Farm has some nice outbuildings, as does Pear Tree Farm, but the southern by-pass will wreck the setting of Lynn Farmhouse for ever, one of the unfortunate necessities of traffic relief.

Finally to Cardington, the most perfect village near to Bedford, now that

Harrowden Lane, Cardington, by Bernard West

Biddenham is being slowly engulfed. Obviously its preservation owes everything to the Whitbread management, and it is fashionable to call this feudal. One can imagine, however, what its fate would have been without this protection.

Starting at Harrowden Lane we have an excellently detailed sequence of housing in red brick with picturesque clustered chimney stacks, and open views to the south, but with the southern by-pass to the north and all too near. The whole frontage is set off by a well maintained hornbeam hedge. The main element about these houses is the detail at the angle of each gable end where a porch with a bracketed post is inserted, a very attractive feature. Numbers 269, 270 and 271 at the corner of Harrowden Lane are visually important in being at

322-323 Cardington Green, by Bernard West

the entrance to the village, and date from 1673, and their present dereliction is regrettable; so one hopes for private purchase and restoration, although number 269 is still occupied.

The little bridge in Cardington over the Elstow Brook of 1779 was built for Samuel Whitbread I, and although posessing a stumpy elegance, would not be notable but for the evocative name of its designer, John Smeaton. One wonders what he would have thought of the massive construction programme only a few yards away.

Pleasant Place further south on Bedford Road has been sold, but the adjoining

Howard Reading Room, Cardington, by Bernard West

Malting Farm is an attractive eighteenth century composition with unusual glazing. How on earth the Planning Authority allowed the detailing of Holme Oak Green, in between, is incomprehensible, a group of such Disneyesque romanticism that it is shamed by its Georgian neighbours.

With numbers 320 and 322 on the Green we return to the sandstone, similar to that of the church. The houses are built in a kind of vertical crazy paving or cyclopean masonry, and numbers 285 and 287 in Southill Road repeat the design. Did George Highton use up the remains of his random rubble from the church rebuilding, which dressed every stone and must have left a lot of waste?

The buildings are in stark contrast to the almost East Anglian character of Cardington, but not unattractive. Number 319 is a delightful late Georgian cottage, adjoining the King's Arms, which again has been sold. More a restaurant than a 'pub', and with the Exeter Arms gone, Cardington is halfway to the state of being 'dry', a fate affecting so many villages and the result of the breathalyser.

John Howard's house, the north-east corner of what amounts to a very attractive 'close', has been reduced, but still forms an essentially eighteenth century house of three bays, from which extend delightful grounds.

The Parish Hall and Parish Cottage, with their verandah, have marvellous brackets to the arcade columns, churchwarden gothic fenestration, and in the cottage a sort of sub-Butterfield waywardness. There are even *vescia* or almond windows in the gables carried out beautifully in stone, with an outer brick trim. The roofing is in two kinds of slate, Welsh and probably Westmorland, and is the finishing touch to a very jolly little building.

The Bedfordshire Rural Communities Charity is housed in the school of 1848 with a delightful bellcote and limestone dressings to hood moulds, label stops and kneelers. All the roofing is in fish scale tiles which give it a very rich texture.

The adjoining Howard Reading Room of 1894 is again in brick with dressings in a red sandstone and with a cupola of copper, giving a slightly forbidding appearance. The round sandstone framed arches at either end, acting as entrances, make up a good composition. It is interesting to read the record of the opening of the Reading Room in memory of one of the 'untitled nobility'. The work was carried out by Mr J Hannam, foreman builder on the estate, with "the advice of the squire, and the assistance of a provisional committee", there being no mention of an architect as such. Samuel Whitbread III may have had problems with the interpretation of working drawings, but it sounds as if he was adequate as an amateur architect. One has a certain sympathy with Hannam, working as 'pig in the middle' between squire and committee. At least in those days he was spared the intervention of the Planners. One thing which is interesting about the Reading Room is that it has a whiff of Art Nouveau about it, even something of Mackintosh, which of course accords with the date. Samuel III was quite probably abreast or even ahead of current architectural thinking.

The Little House, hardly an appropriate name, is a very distinguished villa, in gault brick with white painted Coadestone trim. It would not be out of place to the north of Regents Park. All the glazing is perfect and original. Number 297, adjoining, is a survivor of the eighteenth century or earlier. After School and Reading Room Mr Finlay's Home Farm is a grand Victorian statement tall and

The Little House, Cardington, by Bernard West

assured. There are very attractive if inconvenient outbuildings for which it would be rewarding to find an alternative use.

Numbers 314 to 318 Cople Road are very elegant Georgian cottages, in pebble dash with the happy detail of clear render surrounds to doors and windows, the latter in lead cames. There is the usual roundel, but with the date obliterated, which is a pity. They could be of 1760-70, perhaps the time of the purchase by Samuel I, or perhaps the roundel recorded a Whitbread restoration.

A group of barns further along Cople Road has pantiles of a most attractive texture, with the local detail of the slate courses at the eaves to avoid the problem of rainwater in each row of pantiles surging over the gutter. It is a delightful detail, and with the usual gas tarred weatherboarding below makes a fine group, though sadly probably not functionally ideal for modern farming requirements. It is a good example of the problem of conversion which one meets with attractive old barns. How would one deal with these?

Finally one turns the corner to the Southill Road and more cottages of 1894, the same style as West End Lane, Elstow, and Harrowden Lane. From here one journeys eastward into that slightly melancholy and strangely remote country before climbing the hill to the Warden Abbey plateau. The haunted and forgotten moated site of the old Cardington Manor House lies to the south. One regrets the loss of those great gothic fireplaces and the chimney stack which echoed the design of that on the remnant of the Gostwick Mansion at Old Warden.

The Whitbread achievement has been to produce three oases: at Elstow and at Cardington against the expansion of southern Bedford, and at Southill as a sanctuary of fine trees and an attractive village in a sea of market gardening and rather urbanised landscape.

Chapter 11

The Trees and Woodland

by JOHN NILES

TODAY BEDFORDSHIRE IS not well wooded, and has only five per cent of its land surface under woodland, and nearly half of this is along the Greensand Ridge, a stretch of low hills running from the Leighton Buzzard area north-east across the county. The western parts of Southill and Old Warden are on the ridge, and it is a landscape of woodland and trees with deciduous species as oak, ash and maple, and more recent conifer plantations of pine and larch. The hedgerows, unusually for this county, have many trees along their length and the villages have a wide range of ornamental and unusual trees in the gardens. It is one of the most attractive areas of the county.

Two centuries ago the situation was very different. In Southill and Old Warden, most of the land in the lower-lying east and centre of the parishes was in open arable fields, with the common meadowland lying along the banks of the river Ivel, and in such an open field landscape there were few hedges. Only in the west or on the Ridge proper were there closes, many of medieval origin, bounded by ancient hedgerows containing trees. In these areas were some ancient woodlands, which were the remnants of more extensive ancient forest reduced by assarting (clearance for cultivation) during the later middle ages. Even more recently parts of some woodlands were grubbed up, such as Park Wood and Burnt Wood, which were subsequently let in 1846 to Charles Cole as pasture at 21s per acre. The remaining areas are now among the few surviving ancient woods of outstanding historical and ecological interest in the county.

Management of the older woodlands

These older woodlands were managed largely by coppicing, that is to say, the trees were cut down and the stumps allowed to regrow. The advantages of this system were remarked upon in 1840 by J King in a letter about the sale and thinning of trees at Rowney. He compared the rapidity and cheapness of the regrowth of coppice with the slower and more expensive process of planting afresh. A care-

The Trees and Woodland

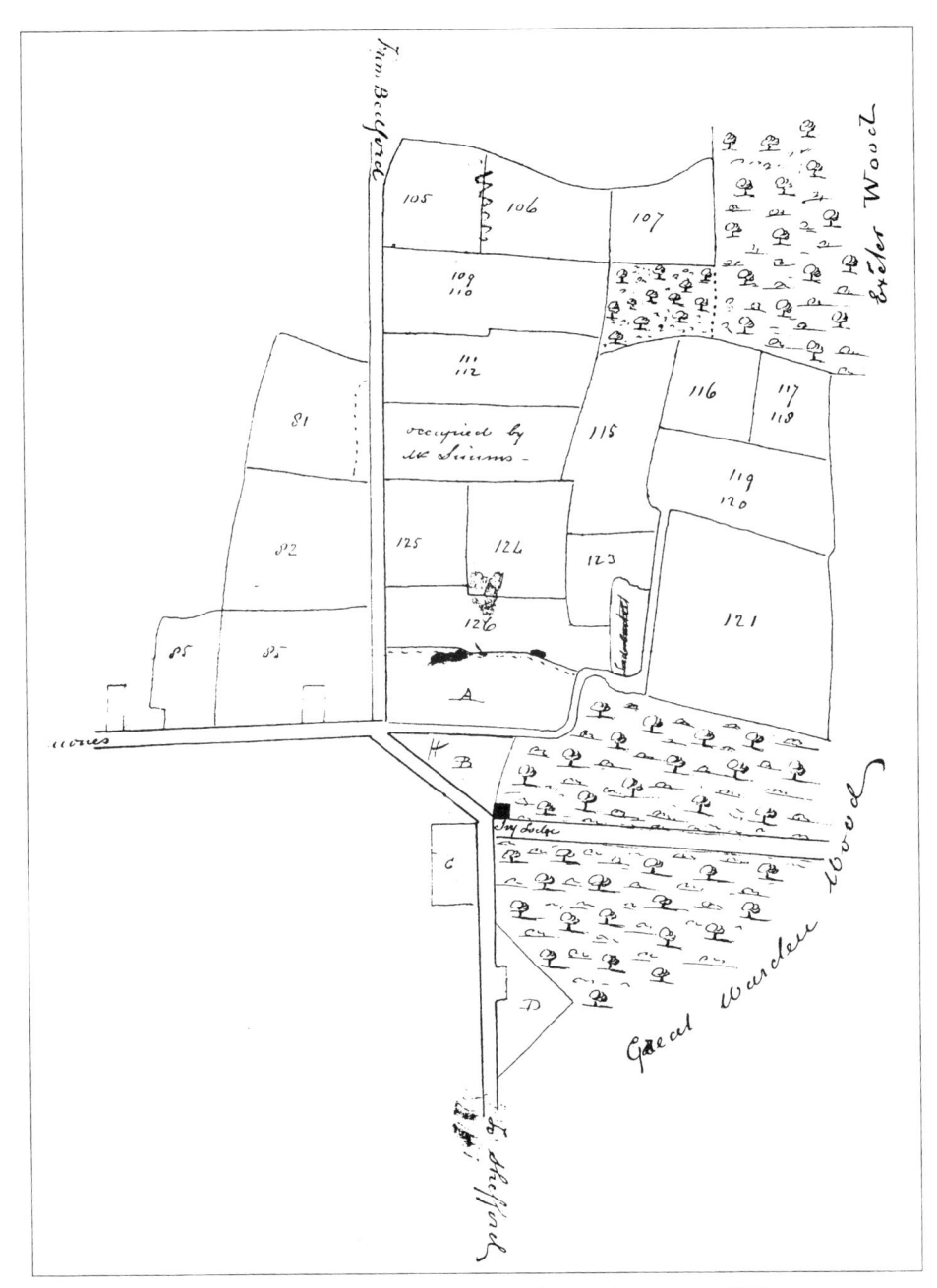

Plan of part of Exeter and Great Warden Woods, August 1843

fully hand-drawn map accompanying details of a lease of Rook Tree Farm of about the same date shows the adjoining part of Exeter and Great Warden Woods. Large symbols represent trees, and smaller ones represent lower growth, and indicate that the wood was managed as coppice with standards. This allowed a mixture of larger timber trees (usually 15 to the acre in the case of oak) and smaller coppice underwood to be grown to provide a wide range of materials.

Before the parliamentary enclosures the remaining land consisted of open arable fields, meadow and rough ground. The woods were a valuable and highly visible resource. The "thriving underwood" is also mentioned. Thomas Batchelor in his *General view of the agriculture of the county of Bedford* of 1808 states that this was cut on a 12/14 year rotation. The woodlands were usually "in hand", that is retained by the landlord and not let to a tenant, and no doubt provided a wide range of wood for estate use as fencing, hurdles, firewood, poles for buildings and spars for thatching. Bark was also stripped for use in the tanning industry.

In the mid nineteenth century the woods were of value for sporting. Sale particulars of Cardington Wood in 1859 and in 1868 state that it was "well intersected with grass rides, Drives and shooting paths. These woods are celebrated for the quantity of game that can always be reared within". A map of Exeter Wood with the sale particulars shows the Great Riding and Little Riding. The Ridings were made to allow for shooting.

Plantations

John Evelyn is generally credited with the move towards the formation of plantations, and in 1664 he could assert that he had induced landowners to plant millions of trees. There were plantings before the seventeenth century, but they were small and uncommon.

In the English midlands, when extensive areas of heath had been enclosed in the era of parliamentary enclosure, planting was on a larger scale. Batchelor says that at Sandy Warren "A great part . . . has been planted with various species of the fir tribe . . . and it is perhaps the best application that can be made of those hilly sands, which produce nothing except ling in their natural state". A great deal of the lighter, sandier soil was uncultivated and used as grazing, or had already been used for creating the medieval warrens. The vegetation on this lighter soil was heathland and consisted of fern and furze (bracken and gorse). This was an ideal habitat for rabbits, and although warrens were not exclusively used for rabbits (they were for ground game) they certainly supported many. As early as 1763 Lord Ongley was proposing the destruction of Warden Warren to convert it to pasture, arable or woodland. However, the heath did supply useful products. Local people were allowed to cut fern and furze to be used as litter or fuel, and it was used also as fuel by bakers, lime burners and brickmakers. Sometimes it was cut on a regular basis like coppice, and was very remunerative. In this county the return was as much as £15 an acre, although Thomas Batchelor tells us that objection was raised to this activity because the furze harboured rabbits "and all kinds of vermin and consequently another deduction from the profits must be made on this account". Nowadays, there is the added problem of depredations by squirrels and deer.

To combine rabbits and heathland vegetation with the growing of trees was extremely difficult and expensive. Rabbits ate the young trees, and the competition from vigorous birch, furze (gorse), and broom severely affected tree growth. All this changed after the enclosure movement of the late eighteenth century. Individual ownership of land allowed areas to be fenced and rabbits controlled. In Bedfordshire in Heath and Reach and Aspley Guise as well as at Sandy Warren (mentioned above) the old sandy heath land seemed to be of little use except as a site for plantations of faster growing coniferous trees, and new groves and coverts were soon established. However, even in 1979 a note in the Southill Estate management plan comments that Keepers' Warren was "weeded every year for 5 years". A heavy infestation of birch coppice and bracken had taken place and the birch scrub had to be taken out in 1986. In the introduction to a "Plan of Operations for the Estate" drawn up in 1972, it states that "the Estate has been in the same ownership since 1793 [sic] but until 1919 no systematic planting was carried out".

This is clearly not the case as most of the existing woodlands had been established long before. Warden Woods were felled during the second world war and replanted with oak and Norway spruce. These are now developing into fine plantations of oak as the spruce are progressively felled and the oak thinned out. Further planting has been done in recent years to restock other areas which have been felled. A considerable amount of new planting has taken place on agricultural land using the various amenity and agricultural incentives which have been available since 1973.

At Southill the changeover from commonfield began early, and most of the new woodlands were laid down shortly after the enclosure had taken place. This can be seen by comparing the pre-enclosure maps with the earliest post enclosure surveys, such as Bryant's printed map of Bedfordshire published in 1826. Today, many of the names of the modern woodland areas can be traced back to the earliest plantings, although some are relatively recent. The area now called Flannels was in 1777 Welbeck Acorns when there was also a Portland Wood, both no doubt named after the Duke of Portland, a close friend of the 4th Viscount Torrington. The estate once bought in seedlings from other nurseries and grew them on in a nursery, but this and other areas are now given over to the production of semi-mature tree stock.

Management of plantations

A letter from James Lilburne, the estate agent, to Samuel Whitbread II dated 17 November 1811 is of particular interest. In it he reports on the thinning of trees at Rowney Warren. The words he uses are revealing. He talks of "... taking down some of the *first* planted Firs by way of thinning them ...". The firs are Scotch Firs, or as we know them Scots Pine (*Pinus sylvestris*). These would have been a natural choice on light, sandy soils. The word 'first' is underlined. As the Enclosure took place in 1800 and there were no woodlands on this piece of land before then, the trees could have been no older than 10 or 11 years. The growth of pine over that period would not have exceeded 5m and this suggests that the trees had established themselves quickly on the site. Bearing in mind the difficulties caused by rabbits and vegetation, this indicates thorough preparation and care of the new plantation. In some areas the ground was cultivated and trees interplanted with agricultural crops to help clean the ground, although there is no indication that this happened here. The trees would have been planted close together to justify thinning them out at such an early stage and the produce would have been quite small. E W Jones in his article entitled *British Forestry in 1790-1813* notes that "... the spacing was often close; 5000 plants per acre (3ft x 3ft) and even closer spacings were not rare. Thinning began early when the trees were 7-8 ft. tall. The markets for small material made these close spacings economically possible".

On 9 May 1840, thirty years later, J King (who was employed by the estate) mentions that "... about 590 feet [presumably Hoppus Feet, a measure of timber volume] of the best Larch sold to Mr Hemmingway". Clearly, though, the thinning of Rowney was overdone. King warns in the same letter that as a result of too frequent fellings it is likely that commitments to customers will not be met in future. Nowadays the Scots pine would be replaced by Corsican Pine, a much faster growing tree, although larch is still planted because it supplies a wide range of products useful to the estate. In addition techniques such as ride widening and the use of tree shelters instead of fencing help to improve conditions for wildlife and improve the shooting.

One of the more accessible woodlands, 183 acres at Rowney Warren, was leased in 1954 to Forest Enterprise for 200 years. There is unlimited public access and it is now a very popular area for walking. In addition, the woods are recognised as of exceptional wildlife interest. Stanford Pit, 59 acres, is also leased to Forest Enterprise until 2154, and is available for fishing.

The Trees and Woodland

Hedgerows and Groves: Triangles and Diamonds

Before the era of parliamentary enclosure it is thought that about three quarters of the area of the county was under the open or common field system of cultivation. Following the enclosures of the various parishes many miles of hedges were planted, and these required large quantities of thorn plants. Thomas Batchelor tells us that on heavy soils a deep ditch was constructed on one side, and a bank on the other. A double row of whitethorn quicks was planted on a ledge in the bank. There were usually two rows of quicks, twelve inches apart, with trees at 5 or 6 inches in the row, and these were protected by a post and rail fence for up to six or seven years. The cost of this was about 10s 6d per pole (or £2.10 for 20m). Nowadays it would cost about £50 for the same length. It was not usual to plant trees in these new fences, although there were exceptions, and Batchelor says that "A few trees of various kinds are sometimes planted in the corners of fields".

Triangles and diamonds along the Southill hedgerows on A. Bryant's map of Bedfordshire of 1826

THE TREES AND WOODLAND

If there was a general reluctance to plant in hedgerows this did not seem to apply at Southill, and the 25 inch Ordnance Survey maps of 1881/2 clearly show individual trees along the hedge lines as well as additional long, narrow belts. Trees were also planted in the area between Broom and Stanford shortly after the enclosure. The points at which the new field boundaries intersected were planted with trees. They first appear on an estate map of 1818 and as the fields were regular in shape, these plantings occur as triangles and diamonds. They still exist and are shown on modern maps and aerial photographs exactly as on early maps. The groups consist now of oak, which survive from the original plantings, but some contain Scots pine. Because of their small size and the fact that the symbols on early maps represent deciduous trees, the pine must have been planted later in place of the oak. These unusual features occur also in smaller numbers near Astwick and Arlesey, but nowhere else. The tradition of hedgerow planting continues to this day and along with the remnants of those early plantings there are new trees, which are very much a feature of this area.

Ornamental trees

The tree belts and groves within Southill Park itself have changed much over the past two hundred years, and are worth investigation. However, it is often the planting of specimen trees within that framework which best reflect the personal taste of the landowner, and at Southill there are many fine and unusual trees. In particular, there are several fastigiate oak near the sawmill. One of these is a Bedfordshire champion. A large layered beech in the garden and specimens of Ponderosa and Monterey pine are unusual for this area.

A collection of cedars in the park to the west of Southill House is of particular note. An undated drawing referring to trees west of the Icehouse was discovered, and it contains the measurements of a number of the trees. Those that survive have recently been remeasured. As a result there are for some trees four sets of measurements between 1908 and 1995. The largest so far is a Cedar of Lebanon with a diameter of 222 cms. New trees have been planted over the past years to maintain the avenue, and this collection continues to be a remarkable feature of Southill Park.

Timber production

The sale of timber has always been a significant part of the Estate economy. In 1916 £10,000 worth was sold to the Home Grown Timber Committee, presumably a government body. Many trees were blown down in the 'North Gale' on 28 March 1916 and an additional 208 oaks, elms and ash trees were felled on the

Timber waggons near Cotton End, c.1930

instruction of the Admiralty, all for the War effort. Regular fellings have taken place over the years and have been sold to such well known local firms as Astell and Perridge. In 1945 there is the first recorded sale of willows to Edgar Watts, specialists in cricket bat production.

The Sawmill

The estate has had a sawmill since before the second world war. The usefulness of the mill is reflected in the accounts for the period July 1960 – March 1976. These list the supply of oak posts and rails to local tenants and farms; softwood for poles; stakes for fencing; material for pheasant pens and estate repairs on the Home Farm and Southill House. In addition, the workshop was able to make up gates, potato boxes and interwoven fencing. A 'Hot and Cold' creosoting plant, fired by offcuts from the mill, was added in order to preserve the timber of pine and other species not naturally durable. Until then, sweet chestnut and larch, which are durable, were used. The first entry for "50 Creosoted Scots piles at £12.50" occurs in May 1972. A further entry, "Tree Stakes (Celurised)" shows the arrival of a modern pressure treatment plant using chemically based preservatives. It was such an innovation that for a while a number of importing companies brought their timber for treatment from as far afield as Yarmouth docks. The old, redundant creosote tanks now lie safely beneath the present sawmill office.

Originally the sawmill had a steam driven circular-saw bench. In 1978/9 the yard was concreted, two extensions built and a Stenner band resaw and a cross-cutting machine installed. The logs were lifted on to a log haul by a Highland Bear tractor and crane unit. In 1986/7 the mill machinery was in need of extensive repair and modernisation, and was temporarily closed for sawmilling. It now operates as an independent enterprise and buys in most of its round timber. There is a flourishing sales department providing a wide range of wood products which include peelings sold for equestrian use. It specialises in sawn and round agricultural fencing, and can offer a complete 'supply and erect' contract fencing service.

It is possible that the estate woodlands may be able to supply more of the mill's requirements directly in ten or fifteen years when the recent plantings are first thinned.

The future of the woodlands

Trees and woodlands have always been an essential element in the estate landscape and economy. This will continue to be the case and although opportunities for extensive new planting are unlikely to occur, the maintenance of the existing trees and woodlands, now such a familiar feature of the landscape of this part of the county, will remain a priority.

Chapter 12

The Estate Today

by SAM WHITBREAD

IN SOME RESPECTS the estate has changed relatively little over the past two hundred years. It has been reduced in area from 12,000 acres in 1815 to 10,800 acres today, largely due to the inexorable growth of Bedford. The spread of the county town was foreseen by successive generations of Whitbreads. In fact, the reason given for the rebuilding of Cardington Church between 1897 and 1901 to the size it is today was to accommodate the expected growth of the parish as Bedford spread south-east. As it happened, Bedford was to spread north-west and north-east and it is only the coming of the by-pass that has heralded the expected expansion of Cardington and Elstow.

The basic income of the estate has, for two hundred years, been largely dependent on rents from farms and cottages. In this respect we continue to follow the advice of Samuel Whitbread I when he wrote in 1793 "English land is the only security and best to live on the income of it if proprietors will submit to the interest it brings which scarce any body will do".

With the estate so dependent on rents, its prosperity has risen and fallen over the years in time with the rises and falls in the prosperity of farming. There have been standstills in rent increases at times when inflation has meant a steady increase in the estate's costs. On the other hand the state of the private housing market has sometimes led to an increased demand for rented accommodation.

The realities of the commercial world have penetrated two departments in particular during the last thirty years. The sawmills, which traditionally converted timber off the estate into fencing for the estate farms, has in recent years expanded considerably, buying-in timber from all over the country and even from abroad, and manufacturing a range of fencing, gates, sheds and other buildings to the value of £500,000 a year delivered far beyond the confines of the estate. Similarly the farm, once just the provider of milk, butter and eggs to Southill House, today covers 1,900 acres and enjoys sales of over £600,000 a year.

At the same time, other departments on the estate employ far fewer people

Garden Party at Southill to celebrate the 200th Anniversary of the Estate, June 1995

than in former times. The builders, who a hundred years ago rebuilt Cardington Church, now number only two, with estate building, maintenance and repair work now being carried out by outside contractors supervised by the estate's building managers. Similarly in the woods, two men are all that is left of a large team (with horses and waggons) who planted, trimmed and felled in days gone by. Again, contractors and machinery have taken their place. In the gardens of Southill House, fourteen were employed until the Second World War. Today, with the old kitchen garden let and labour-saving measures introduced, the work is done by three men.

This trend towards mechanization and labour reduction is echoed on the estate's tenanted farms. In the first half of the century, cottages on the estate were occupied by estate employees or by those working on the tenanted farms. Now, the majority of the cottages are rented by tenants who work in Bedford or Biggleswade, Luton or Letchworth; some even commute daily to London.

Manpower reductions are by no means the only feature of the estate's recognition of the need to modernize if it is to survive. Farm tenants are encouraged to seek non-agricultural uses for farm buildings not required for farming purposes. Efforts are made to let redundant farm buildings to small businesses under business tenancies. Alternative uses (other than residential) have been sought for larger houses situated close to Bedford, resulting in an increased income for the estate, whose declared policy is to maximize the estate's income while retaining the traditional principles and framework of a country estate. At the same time attempts have been made to reduce the estate's dependence on the fluctuating fortunes of British agriculture; non-agricultural income now accounts for half of the total income of the estate.

Samuel Charles Whitbread receiving the Bledisloe Gold Medal from H.M. The Queen at the Royal Show, 1989

In addition to providing employment for around seventy people, together with that of a number of contractors, the estate is also conscious of its responsibility to the local community. Support is given to the village shops in Southill and Elstow, and consideration is given to the needs of village schools through the policy of letting houses to young couples. Other community facilities – halls, social clubs and sporting facilities – are provided in return for nominal rents.

In 1989 the Southill Estate was awarded the Bledisloe Gold Medal by the Royal Agricultural Society of England. The medal is awarded periodically to a landowner who has "done outstanding service in encouraging the application of science or technology to some branch of British Husbandry" and I was proud to receive the medal from Her Majesty The Queen at the Royal Show in July. In his report in the Society's *Journal* the judge wrote: "The management of Southill displays an awareness of the many and varied resources of the average agricultural estate and the ability to put these to productive and beneficial use. There is a marked concern for the welfare of those who live on the property and those whose proximity to it inevitably involves them with it in one way of another. There is a willingness to share the resources of the estate with them for the benefit of the whole, but there is no element of the patrician in administration and management".

With the possible exception of the final phrase, I would like to think that these words could have been written about the Southill Estate at any time during my family's two hundred years of occupation.